The British
Economic Disaster

The British
Economic Disaster

Andrew Glyn
and John Harrison

Pluto Press

First published 1980 by Pluto Press Limited,
Unit 10 Spencer Court, 7 Chalcot Road, London NW1 8LH

Copyright © Andrew Glyn and John Harrison 1980

ISBN 0 86104 317 0

Photoset and printed in Great Britain by Photobooks (Bristol) Limited,
28 Midland Road, St Philips, Bristol

Cover illustration by Peter Kennard
Cover design by Marsha Austin

Contents

Contents

Contents

Acknowledgements

This book grew out of work done with Philip Armstrong. Many of the ideas are his. We would also like to thank the following for helping us to write it: Caroline Baldwin, Eva Kaluzynska, Richard Kuper, Sybil Owen, Phillipe Van Parys, Bob Rowthorn and Caroline Wise.

Introduction: Modern Times

The decade we have just emerged from was crucial for the British left. For many, including ourselves, whose memories stretch back only to the fifties, and whose radicalisation dates from the late sixties, it was a period of political baptism. And what a period it was.

The seventies opened with the election of a Tory government well to the right of any since the war. It closed with the election of one which makes its predecessor seem middle of the road. Between the two, Labour ruled. It gained office on a programme well to the left of any adopted for a quarter of a century. Yet its policies in government attacked jobs and living standards more effectively than those of its Tory predecessor.

In the early 1970s more workers took to the streets to defend living standards and trade union rights than at any time since the twenties. Industrial action brought down a government for the first time in British history. By contrast, in the middle years of the decade, the labour movement seemed resigned to its official party implementing policies that brought the largest fall in living standards recorded this century and mass unemployment on a scale close to that of the thirties.

At the end of the sixties, the Labour Party seemed to many to be firmly established as a respectable party of government, likely in coming years to alternate with the Tories in a Tweedledum and Tweedledee act in which one performer could barely be distinguished from the other. Yet by the end of the seventies the party, as represented by annual conference, was committed to a thorough-going process of internal democratisation and a radical left-wing programme. It was at war with its parliamentary leadership.

Underlying all this was a sharp deterioration in British capital's performance. The best single indicator of the intensifying economic difficulties is the collapse in the rate of profit, which fell from about 12 per cent in the early sixties to some 4 per cent in the late seventies. If the pundits are right, it will be down to 2 per cent in 1980.

So it is hardly surprising that employment in the manufacturing backbone of the economy fell throughout the decade, that around one in ten people is now out of work and production is falling. Nor should it come as a great surprise that the traditional workers' party, whose rationale during the fifties and sixties was the ability to offer reforms to workers without endangering the fabric of capitalism, has been catapulted into a state of crisis.

We have emerged from the seventies only in the formal sense of having turned the page on a calendar. The key features of the decade remain with us today, and are likely to continue well into the eighties. This book, which is basically about the relation between economic and political developments in the UK during the seventies, is intended as a contribution to learning the lessons of those years.

The focus on economic matters should not be taken to indicate that we believe them to be the only ones of political importance. We do not. Nor should it be seen as suggesting that the book is for professional economists. It is written by socialists for trade union militants and political activists (though we hope students will also find it useful).

So facts are included which, while familiar to economists, are seldom made easily available to the workers' movement. The use of economic and marxist terminology has been kept to a minimum. Where we use terms unfamiliar to someone who regularly watches TV news bulletins, we explain them briefly the first time they occur. The priority accorded to readability also accounts for our omitting detailed discussion of alternative explanations. (There is a bibliography for readers wishing to consult other accounts.)

The greatest difficulty we found in writing the book was that of devising a suitable structure. The one finally adopted is as follows:

The opening chapters examine the two major determinants of the acute economic difficulties facing British capital: the crisis gripping the international economy (Chapter 1) and the increasing and chronic weakness of the UK relative to major competitors (Chapter 2). The following two chapters then discuss the policies pursued by Tory and Labour governments respectively during the seventies. The final chapter looks ahead to the eighties. It begins with a brief discussion of prospects for the world economy before moving on to assess three possible strategies for regenerating British industry: Thatcherism, the Alternative Economic Strategy and a planned socialist economy.

This structure has two advantages. First, it seems to us to embody the logical order of analysis. Secondly, it is the one within which certain notions we believe essential to an understanding of contemporary developments can best be explained.

But there is a possible disadvantage: readers anxious to come to grips immediately with the rough and tumble of class struggle in the seventies may be impatient with the first two chapters. This reaction would be unfortunate. These chapters are essential to an understanding of the broad sweep of developments within which recent struggles in the UK must be located, and of certain theoretical ideas which underpin the analysis in later chapters (in particular, those of production and realisation and the 'scrapping mechanism'). Nor are these broader developments uninteresting in themselves. They are among the most dramatic and important of modern times.

1.
World Capitalism in Crisis

Limits of the long boom

Between 1952 and 1968, world capitalist output doubled. So almost half the goods and services regularly consumed today would not be available but for developments during those 16 post-war years. This achievement is without historical parallel. The long boom of the 1950s and 1960s saw the most rapid and sustained development of production in human history.

The driving force of the boom was the rapid rate at which the stock of machines and factories (means of production) grew. (See Table 1 below.)

1: Long-run Growth in Advanced Capitalist Countries

	Rate of growth of output per head of population	Rate of growth of stock of means of production
	Average annual percentage	
1870–1913	1.5	2.8
1913–1950	1.1	1.6
1950–1970	3.8	5.6

Source: Maddison 1977, Table 6.

Growth in this stock raises output. Workers equipped with more and better machinery produce more. Labour productivity rises.

Under capitalism, machines and factories are owned by

individual companies, which employ workers and organise production. The capitalists who control these companies are in business to make money. They are not interested in high labour productivity as a goal in itself, and do not install more machinery unless they believe they can raise their profits by doing so.

During a boom, capitalists stock up with machinery, or *accumulate capital*, because they are confident this will yield rewards. So an examination of a capitalist boom such as that of the fifties and sixties must focus on the relationship between profits and accumulation.

Production, realisation, accumulation and profits

The whole purpose of production, from the point of view of capitalists, is to make a profit. They do this by putting workers to work. The results are distributed as follows.

Some of the product has to replace machinery worn out and materials used up. Some of it is paid out to workers in the form of wages. The rest is the surplus. It is surplus from the workers' point of view because they are forced to produce it, but cannot afford to buy it with their wages. This portion is the source of profit. Its value is known as *surplus value*.

Several factors determine how much surplus value is produced. A worker's output over any given time affects the outcome. Efficient, intensive production methods mean higher labour productivity than sloppy, slow ones. The proportion of the product paid out in wages influences the size of the surplus too. Plainly, the lower the wage, the larger the surplus. Finally, the cost of importing raw materials can tip the balance for or against a satisfactory yield for the capitalist.

Even if conditions for producing surplus value are favourable, capitalists do not actually pocket profits unless they sell their produce. The amount of profit they make depends not only on the conditions for producing surplus value, but also on those for selling products, or *realising* surplus value.

Conditions for realising surplus value are favourable when demand for commodities is high, for then it is possible to sell a lot and at high prices. Demand may be high because the government, workers or capitalists at home are spending heavily, or because exports are selling well.

The amount of surplus value produced can, of course, fall short of the potential possible when the system is working flat out. If workers are on the dole and machinery is idle, actual surplus value falls short of potential surplus value. This will happen if capitalists believe they could not sell more without cutting prices and reducing profits; in other words, it will occur if realisation conditions are poor.

Accumulation and profits are related in a complex way. If profits are high, capitalists are encouraged to invest in more machines. So favourable conditions for producing and realising surplus value encourage accumulation. But accumulation itself tends to generate good conditions.

With new machinery, labour productivity rises, improving conditions for producing surplus value. Spending on investment means markets expand, improving conditions for realisation. For as long as the boom lasts, actual surplus value matches potential fairly closely.

So once a boom gets going it is largely self-sustaining. Understanding why it starts involves discovering how favourable conditions are first established. Understanding why it comes to an end – which is what we are mainly interested in here – involves discovering how it is undermined, how one or more of the conditions becomes unfavourable.

In the fifties and sixties a high rate of accumulation, and with it favourable conditions for producing and realising surplus value, were facilitated by adequate supplies of labour and a rapid growth in world trade.

Supplies of labour

The rate at which the stock of means of production grew (*the rate of accumulation*) was nearly 6 per cent a year during the boom. But employment in the advanced capitalist countries grew by only about 1 per cent a year. There was a rapid rise in the amount of equipment per worker (what Marx called the *technical composition of capital*). A modest rate of employment growth thus proved adequate and, at least until the early sixties, labour markets were slack enough to prevent real wages rising sufficiently to jeopardise conditions favourable for producing surplus value. So why is the issue of labour supply important?

A low rate of recruitment to a labour force already fully employed is seldom sufficient to maintain a high rate of accumulation, even if the amount of machinery per worker rises sharply. A period of rapid accumulation invariably involves extremely fast growth in dynamic leading sectors. These often require massive influxes of labour. Large-scale, swift recruitment into key industries is almost impossible in a tight labour market. There has to be an abundant supply of potential workers (what Marx called the *reserve army of labour*) if there are to be big, quick shifts in employment patterns.

In Japan, for example, employment in the construction industry nearly doubled between 1955 and 1961, rising by more than a million. In electrical engineering employment trebled from a quarter to three quarters of a million over the same period. Such increases would have been impossible without large reserves of potential labour.

The workers who conveniently appeared just when needed were not an abnormally large crop of school-leavers. The growth of employment overall was almost twice as fast as that of the indigenous population of working age in the advanced capitalist (or metropolitan) countries. The 'extra' workers were found in several ways.

One source important in the early fifties was a large pool of unemployed – in W. Germany, Japan and Italy in particular. Registered unemployment in both W. Germany and Italy fell by over a million during the fifties. By the end of the decade, however, large-scale open unemployment had been eliminated almost everywhere except the US.

Net immigration boosted the working population, especially in Europe where in most countries it peaked in the fifties, stayed high during the early sixties, then tapered off towards the end of the decade as immigration controls tightened. By 1969, 6–7 per cent of the labour force in France, W. Germany and Italy were immigrant workers.

The number of married women working outside the home also rose sharply. This shift became significant in the late sixties and continued into the early seventies. The proportion of the female population (aged between 25 and 64) out at work rose in the US from 40 per cent in 1960 to 48 per cent in 1970. In France, to take a European case, it went up from 42 to 47 per cent in the same period.

Finally, growth of total employment is only part of the story. The number of wage labourers employed by capital grew considerably faster than total employment. Wage workers accounted for 68 per cent of employment in the advanced capitalist world in 1954 and 81 per cent in 1973. Accumulation in the modern industrial sector, in which most investment took place, therefore required and absorbed a large number of people previously self-employed. Between 1954 and 1973, this shift out of self-employment accounted for half the increase in the number of wage labourers.

Among the previously self-employed looking for work were those hit by the decline of pre-capitalist manufacturing concerns, especially in textiles and clothing, as companies using modern techniques drove their predecessors out of business.

The decline of peasant-based agriculture was the other major source of workers for modern industry. In 1954, 22 per cent of the metropolitan labour force was working on farms. A mass exodus from agriculture started in the 1950s and continued throughout the 1960s. This was the largest single factor boosting the urban labour force in both Italy and Japan during the 1960s. By 1973, only 8 per cent of the metropolitan labour force remained on farms.

Modern industry would not have been able to sustain the high rate of accumulation which characterised the fifties and sixties without these extra sources of labour. The boom instigated the destruction of pre-capitalist forms of production, then absorbed the workers displaced – a classic process of proletarianisation.

Growth of trade

Developments in world trade during the boom are summarised in Table 2 below. There are three major features of the period. They are the historically unprecedented rate of growth of world trade, the extent to which the growth was concentrated in manufactures, and its increasingly intrametropolitan nature. These factors played a crucial role in stimulating accumulation.

2: Growth of Trade

a. Rate of growth of exports	Average annual percentage
1870–1913	3.7
1913–1950	1.1
1950–1970	8.6

	Indices (1938 = 100)	
b. Trade volume by type of good	1950	1970
Manufactures	125	720
Primary products	90	210

c. Trade between metropolitan countries as a percentage of total trade

1953	33
1970	52

Sources: Barratt-Brown 1972, pp. 103, 119; Maddison 1977, Table 6.

In the late forties, the proportion of output traded between advanced capitalist economies was extremely small by historical standards. A vast structure of tariffs and quotas had been erected during the thirties and the war, behind which internationally uncompetitive and ossified sectors co-existed with modern, competitive ones. There was considerable variation between countries as to which industries fell into which category. But most economies were a combination of modern, dynamic industries, in which accumulation was concentrated, and some backward, semi-stagnant ones, in which little accumulation took place.

The progressive removal of trade restrictions helped provide conditions favourable to both the production and realisation of surplus value. Labour productivity rose, helping to ensure an adequate rate of potential surplus value. And markets expanded, enabling surplus value to be realised. The processes worked as follows.

With foreign markets opening up, internationally competitive leading sectors within a national economy were able to export goods, expanding sales more rapidly than internal demand permitted. This provided them with an incentive to expand their production base faster too. The expansion of trade stimulated a high rate of investment. Rapid growth of investment expenditure, an important part of demand for commodities, was also essential to provide the right conditions for realisation.

Internationally uncompetitive, backward industries conceded defeat in competition with the newly admitted imports. A new, constantly evolving international division of labour emerged. Workers within each national economy became increasingly concentrated in sectors in which labour productivity was comparatively high in international terms.

The high rate of accumulation in dynamic sectors, made possible by their expansion into foreign markets, also stepped up their rate of productivity growth. The Japanese motor and electronics industries are good examples of sectors in which foreign trade permitted a huge expansion of volume, progressive improvement of mass production techniques and hence a tremendous rise in labour productivity. Such a rise was essential to maintain conditions favourable for producing surplus value.

Over-accumulation in the late sixties

By the second half of the sixties, capitalism found it could not sustain the rate of accumulation it had previously achieved. There was *over-accumulation in relation to the supply of labour*. Despite mass unemployment in peripheral (mainly ex-colonial) countries, and millions of women in metropolitan centres still not out at work, capital was starved of labour. Why?

The explanation is that the labour supply is socially constrained under capitalism. So a labour shortage is perfectly possible while potential immigrants are queueing for entry permits refused for political reasons, women are compelled to stay at home looking after children because there are no child care facilities, and capitalists hesitate to invest in countries with a labour surplus for fear of expropriation by radical regimes. This is precisely what happened in Europe and Japan in the late sixties.

In our opinion, over-accumulation was the basic cause of the major fall in profitability and the rise in inflation which occurred from the mid-sixties. (There is a further discussion of explanations for the fall in profitability in the Appendix.)

Reasonably reliable data on the rate of profit (the percentage return capitalists receive on average on the money they lay out to buy machines, pay wages, and so on) has been published only recently. The best available official estimates are summarised in Table 3 together with our calculations for countries for which satisfactory official data are not available.

3. Rates of Profit for Industrial and Commercial Companies

| | Percentages before tax | | | | |
	1960	1965	1970	1973	1975
UK	14.2	11.8	8.7	7.2	3.5
USA	9.9	13.7	8.1	8.6	6.9
France	11.9	9.9	11.1	10.2	4.1
Japan	19.7	15.3	22.7	14.7	9.5
Italy*	11.0	7.9	8.6	4.5	0.8
Germany*	23.4	16.5	15.6	12.1	9.1

Source: Clark and Williams; Feldstein and Summers: Delestre and Mairesse; Annual Report on National Income Statistics of Japan, 1979.
Estimates for Italy and Germany based on national account and capital stock sources are very rough and cannot be compared with those of other countries.

Over-accumulation in relation to the supply of labour means a fall in profitability. This fall can be brought about by various mechanisms (see Appendix). The simplest is the following:

Capitalists instal new machinery but they find there are not enough extra workers available to operate it all. Competition between firms for scarce labour bids up real wages. As pay goes up, older, less productive machinery is *scrapped* (i.e. withdrawn from use), because it can no longer be operated profitably at the higher real wage level, and workers are sacked. Real wages rise until sufficient scrapping occurs to release enough workers from old machinery to operate all the new. The rate of profit falls. This process can be referred to as the *scrapping mechanism*.

It is in principle possible for the scrapping mechanism to operate in a way which does not disrupt the system. Wages could rise, scrapping accelerate and the rate of surplus value and accumulation fall smoothly until the latter was reduced to a level permanently sustainable, given the rate at which the labour force grows. But this is not what happened in the late sixties, when over-accumulation gave rise to the crisis of the seventies. Why?

From over-accumulation to crisis

Trade unions and class struggle

The above outline of the scrapping mechanism implicitly assumes a competitive labour market, in which wages balance supply and demand for workers; it ignores collective bargaining. This simplification was made to show clearly how real wages must rise and the rate of profit fall when over-accumulation occurs. The fall in profits was basically due to the internal dynamics of the accumulation process rather than action on the part of workers' organisations.

But trade unions were by no means irrelevant. Indeed, their power and influence increased with the onset of over-accumulation because greater demand for labour improved their bargaining position over pay.

In the late sixties, there was a remarkable wave of worker/ student strikes, demonstrations and occupations and a number of 'wage explosions' took place. 1968 saw the historic May events in France. 1969 witnessed an outbreak of wild-cat strikes in W. Germany. Wages shot up in the Netherlands and Italy had a 'Hot Autumn'.

The headlines captured a series of dramatic manifestations of class struggle, but seldom gauged the intensifying economic difficulties underlying them. The Organisation for Economic

Cooperation and Development (OECD), speaking for the guardians of the system, wrote of a 'sense of unease to which the discord in labour markets – and in the streets – had given rise'.

The form these struggles took varied from country to country, influenced by factors such as the histories of the labour movements involved and the national political contexts. But most shared an important feature. They were largely the product of rank and file pressure. Trade union leaders, whose perspectives were limited to gradual improvements in pay and conditions, were generally drawn in reluctantly and tried to tone down the scale of demands and the extent of action in support of them.

The money-wage increases won in many cases exceeded considerably the level required for scrapping purposes (given the existing rate of inflation). Conditions for producing surplus value deteriorated further and the system's chances of adjusting smoothly to the onset of labour shortage grew slimmer.

Uneven development and the world monetary crisis

The breakdown of the international monetary system, which occurred at about the same time, also added to the system's adjustment problems and influenced the form of the crisis brought on by over-accumulation.

The interrelation between developments in accumulation and those in the international financial system is a complex one. A stable international payments system was an essential precondition for the enormous expansion of world trade during the boom, in turn essential to the scale of accumulation achieved. But the major economies registered very different rates of accumulation. The rate in Japan was about four times that in the US, for example (see Table 4 below). This unevenness undermined and eventually destroyed the international monetary system on which accumulation had been based.

The principles of the international payments system were established at the Bretton Woods Conference in 1944. The US dollar, which constituted the main form of international money, was convertible into gold on demand at a fixed rate. The rates at which other currencies exchanged against the dollar, and hence against each other, were also pegged within an extremely narrow band. But they could be altered from time to time by devaluation or revaluation against the dollar.

The US was able to establish the dollar as the main form of international money because of its enormous strength relative to other capitalist powers. During post-war reconstruction, Europe and Japan were starved of essential commodities such as food, materials and fuel, many of which could be obtained only from dollar-bloc economies. In this situation there was no question of capitalists or governments finding dollars an unacceptable form of payment and their convertibility into gold was of little practical importance. The dollar was more secure than Fort Knox.

But things had changed by the late sixties. The most obvious manifestation of the system's weakness was a series of exchange rate adjustments, beginning with the devaluation of sterling in November 1967. But these exchange rate changes were only symptoms of the underlying malady: the decline of the dollar. The disease turned out to be fatal. The Bretton Woods system survived an attack of speculation in the summer of 1971 only in a crippled form. A second, even more feverish, episode in spring 1973 proved terminal.

The fundamental reason for the decline of the dollar was the growth of the US balance of payments deficit during the sixties. In the mid-sixties, US exports exceeded imports, but there was an outflow on capital account – comprising government expenditure abroad (aid, military spending) and foreign investment by US capital (building factories and buying financial assets overseas). For the sixties as a whole, the overall deficit totalled more than $30 billion.

Foreign governments and capitalists financed almost the entire deficit by increased holdings of dollars. They were prepared to retain dollars received from US capital in payment for commodities or assets because of the interest paid on them. These dollars could theoretically be cashed in for gold. But as foreign dollar holdings grew, it became increasingly obvious that there was not enough gold in Fort Knox to cover them all. The problem intensified in the early seventies as the US trade balance moved into deficit – a development which added to the flood of dollars abroad.

The onset of a deficit on trade in goods was the result of the relative decline of the US economy. Production techniques improved considerably more rapidly in Europe and Japan during this period than in the US. American capital became decreasingly competitive internationally. By 1973, the US was involved in only 33 per cent of world capitalist investment, as compared with 64 per cent in 1950, while Japan's share had risen from 4 per cent to 22 per cent and that of the original EEC Six from 17 per cent to 34 per cent.

In 1971, there was massive speculation against the dollar. Capitalists transferred their money from dollars into strong currencies, such as the Deutschmark, which they expected would rise in value. The German and other central banks were forced to buy enormous quantities of dollars to hold down their exchange rates. Their dollar reserves rose in that single year by almost twice as much as in the whole of the previous ten years. In August 1971, Nixon abandoned dollar/gold convertibility.

A new set of exchange rates was established by the Smithsonian Agreement of December 1971, which included a 9 per cent devaluation of the dollar. But this agreement – described by Nixon as 'the most significant monetary agreement in the history of the world' – lasted just 14 months. As the US deficit worsened, speculation increased and by March 1973 all major currencies were floating against the dollar. The Bretton Woods system was dead and buried.

However, the break-up of the Bretton Woods system has not as yet seriously disrupted the pattern of world trade. Its most important role to date has been to fuel the inflationary forces generated by over-accumulation. (See pp. 19–20 below.)

Inflation and the development of the crisis

Prices rose extremely slowly in the late fifties and early sixties. Only from the mid-sixties onwards did inflation become significant and regarded as a major cause for concern. The rate at which prices went up was one of the first indications that capitalism might not adjust smoothly to labour shortage.

Widespread inflation was primarily due to over-accumulation. Because real wages went up, workers were able to spend more. Since labour shortage prevented production from rising, inflation could have been avoided only if either investment or state expenditure had been reduced correspondingly. But they were not. State spending continued to rise at least as rapidly as tax revenues (considerably more so in the US, which was becoming heavily committed to the war in South East Asia) and capital did not cut back investment significantly.

Capital's attempt to continue accumulating at a rate it could no longer sustain permanently was in most cases temporarily successful in the late sixties. The rate of accumulation was checked in W. Germany and Italy but generally maintained elsewhere. It even rose in the US. (See Table 4 below.)

4: Rates of Accumulation 1950–73

Growth rate of gross capital stock, industry and services

| | Average annual percentages | | | | | |
	France	Italy	Germany	UK	US	Japan
1950–60	3.3	5.7	6.9	2.8	3.4	5.0
1960–65	5.6	7.2	8.1	4.0	3.5	12.0
1965–70	5.9	5.0	6.7	4.2	4.7	13.0
1970–73	6.1	4.9	6.9	3.8	4.0	12.9

Source: Economie et Statistique, *September 1979 (France);* Bolletino Mensile di Statistica, *January 1978 (Italy): Deutsches Institut fur Wirtschaftsforschung, Berlin (various publications), (Germany);* National Income and Expenditure *(UK);* Survey of Current Business *(US); Economic Planning Agency (Japan).*

So accumulation held up for a while despite the labour shortage, and strained the system considerably. All available machines were being used to capacity, but capital was still incapable of supplying enough commodities to satisfy demand at existing prices. Hence inflation.

This primary impetus for inflation was reinforced by wage explosions, which encouraged capitalists to push up prices, trying to maintain profitability in spite of soaring wage bills.

The 1970–71 recession

By the end of 1969, the rate of inflation in the advanced capitalist world had risen to 5 per cent a year compared with 2.8 per cent a year between 1960 and 1968. In 1968 and 1969, governments almost everywhere responded to inflation, and to the accompanying wage explosions, by cutting spending and imposing tight money policies; that is, by restrictive *demand-management* policies. The result was a significant recession.

Industrial production in the capitalist world grew at an annual rate of only ¾ per cent between the early months of 1970 and the close of 1971. The proportion of plant and machinery (*fixed capital*) gathering dust worldwide began to rise from the beginning of 1969. Unemployment began to rise from the end of 1969. By the end of 1971, it had increased by about a third. Some 3½ per cent of the labour force was out of work.

The recession affected production and employment more than prices. The rate of inflation worldwide fell only slightly to a low point of just over 4 per cent a year in the winter of 1971–72. The widespread notion that the principal difference between the present crisis and previous ones is stagflation – the coexistence of recession and inflation – originates from this period.

The mini-boom of 1971–73

1972 and 1973 were boom years in all advanced capitalist economies. Between the first half of 1972 and that of 1973, world capitalist industrial production shot up by 10 per cent.

The boom was extremely inflationary and speculative. Prices began to accelerate very early on when a substantial amount of machinery was still idle. By the first half of 1973, prices were rising at a rate of 7½ per cent a year.

Speculation initially took place primarily in gold and real estate and then spread to primary products. Between the summer of 1972 and the autumn of 1973, industrial materials prices more or less doubled.

Capitalists' enthusiasm for buying cocoa crops yet to be harvested and holding empty office space was not accompanied by an irresistible urge to instal more machinery. Total investment grew at more or less the same rate as during the previous and much gentler boom, but in the crucial manufacturing sector was considerably more sluggish in a number of countries.

The effects of the boom on unemployment were also limited. Jobless totals began to fall from around the turn of 1971–72, but remained high by sixties standards. At the low point reached in the autumn of 1973 unemployment stood at about 3 per cent of the labour force.

These features of the boom were the result of a number of developments. Governments in all major capitalist countries had responded to the 1970–71 recession by implementing expansionary demand management policies. These reflationary measures were generally introduced in 1971 and maintained or expanded during 1972. They had two distinctive characteristics. First, the package was highly synchronised internationally; it was introduced more or less simultaneously in all major capitalist economies. Secondly, the measures consisted of increases in the money supply and reductions in interest rates rather than additions to state expenditure or cuts in taxation. That is, it was more a monetary than a fiscal package.

Because the preceding recession had been comparatively synchronised, the application of 'conventional' economic criteria to determine appropriate demand-management policies within each country would itself tend to produce synchronised expansion. In addition, a number of major elections took place in 1972. There was a US presidential election as well as elections for the principal legislative assemblies in Canada, W. Germany, Italy and Japan – economies which, taken together, produce about 70 per cent of world capitalist output.

A further factor, which not only reinforced synchronisation, but also played a major role in determining the overwhelmingly monetary nature of the package, was the break-up of the international payments system. The scale of the flight from the dollar in the early seventies was such that almost no major capitalist economy was short of dollar reserves.

Between 1960 and 1968, world dollar reserves grew by an average of about 2–3 per cent a year. In 1971, they grew by 43 per cent as capitalists holding dollars cashed them in for other currencies and the dollars piled up as reserves in central bank vaults.

The flight from the dollar led to monetary-based expansion because governments were compelled to print money to buy this vast influx of dollars. The money supply in the capitalist world as a whole grew at a fairly steady rate of about 7 per cent a year between 1963 and 1970. Then it accelerated sharply, growing by some 14 per cent in 1971, 18 per cent in 1972 and 20 per cent in 1973.

Synchronised, monetary-based expansion in an inflationary context could be expected to provoke steeper price rises and speculation in almost any circumstances. In the case of the mini-boom, however, two other factors also played a role.

One is widely acknowledged: unforeseen shortages of food and materials. World cereals production fell by 3 per cent in 1972, largely because of crop failures in the USSR, Australia, China and much of South East Asia.

World food prices rose by $13\frac{1}{2}$ per cent between the first six months of 1972 and those of 1973. Statistically, this rise accounts for more than half of the increase in inflation during that period.

The other factor has had less of an airing, but is nevertheless crucial. Profitability remained low despite increased levels of production and capacity utilisation (see Table 3 above).

Capitalists had discovered that the conditions for realising surplus value had improved spectacularly, while those for producing it had at best remained unsatisfactory. Their response to this situation was a classic one: they sought to make profits in circulation rather than in production. They bought rubber yet to be tapped rather than machinery and sought to exploit the vagaries of the market rather than the labour of the unemployed. This is the fundamental reason why the mini-boom was so inflationary and speculative.

Governments' current obsession with monetary targets stems in large part from the experience of the mini-boom. Having once lost control of the money supply, they have resolved to keep a keen eye on it in future.

The oil crisis

In October 1973, war broke out in the Middle East. The resulting political solidarity among Arab oil-producing states, together with the greater demand for oil which accompanied the mini-boom, gave a new lease of life to the Organisation of Petroleum Exporting Countries (OPEC), a cartel of major oil producers.

OPEC imposed a major price increase. Oil prices quadrupled during winter 1973–74. The oil-producers' annual income rose by around $64 billion, enough money to buy $1\frac{1}{2}$ per cent of world capitalist output. This happened in the context of restrictive demand-management policies, rapidly decelerating growth and double-digit inflation.

All major capitalist governments began to impose restrictive policies in 1973. World-capitalist output decelerated from an annual rate of growth of 8 per cent in the first half of 1973 to 3 per cent in the second half of the year. Unemployment began to rise in the autumn of 1973. But world inflation accelerated to an annual rate of 10 per cent in the second half of the year, as price rises affecting raw materials fed through to the final-goods market and workers sought pay deals large enough to make up for earlier price rises.

The rise in oil prices increased costs. Conditions for producing surplus value deteriorated. The pressure on capitalists to raise prices intensified. Much fixed capital could no longer be operated profitably at existing prices given the increase in fuel costs.

The oil price rise also affected the conditions for realising surplus value adversely. The OPEC countries did not, and indeed in the short-run simply could not, spend much of their extra revenue. World demand therefore fell.

If governments had kept to the demand-management policies then in favour, the oil price rise would have had the following effects. It would have increased the real cost of imported inputs and thus put pressure on capitalists to accelerate price rises in an attempt to restore the conditions for producing surplus value. But conditions for realising surplus value would have deteriorated too. The oil price increase would also have reduced demand, cutting the volume of goods that could be sold at existing, let alone increased, prices. The inevitable outcome would have been a slump.

Governments could have responded by instituting more

expansionary demand-management policies, to allow commodity sales at higher prices. But they did not. Instead, they opted for a more restrictive tack. Monetary policies were further tightened in most economies in the spring of 1974. This aggravated the conditions for realisation and exacerbated the subsequent slump.

Production held up for some months. Output continued to grow in all major economies except the US during the first half of 1974. The oil price rise reactivated the boom in food and materials prices and inflation accelerated, reaching an annual rate of 15 per cent in the spring of 1974. Worldwide inflation of this magnitude was almost unprecedented in peacetime.

Because output held up and prices accelerated at this time, one or both were going to have to come down even more sharply later. The onset of slump was delayed, but its subsequent scale increased.

Many commentators attribute almost all recent economic problems to the oil crisis. This position is untenable. The basic difficulties – over-accumulation in relation to the supply of labour and consequent decline in profitability – were not a result of the oil crisis. They preceded it and would not have evaporated had it never happened. Nor is there any reason to assume that capitalism would have adjusted easily to over-accumulation had there been no oil crisis. Quite the contrary. The feverish character of the mini-boom hardly augured smooth adjustment.

Nor can the slump be blamed on OPEC's failure to spend its increased oil revenues. Governments could perfectly well have offset the reduction in expenditure by adopting expansionary demand-management policies.

Finally, the oil crisis was largely a product of the underlying problems. The price rise was in part prompted by the decline in the value of dollar-dominated OPEC revenues which followed the collapse of the Bretton Woods system. It is also doubtful if OPEC could have imposed and maintained the rise without the high demand for oil which accompanied the mini-boom.

But the oil crisis was far from trivial. It had significant negative effects on conditions for producing and realising surplus value and thus played an important part in bringing about the subsequent slump.

The crash of 1974

There was a major crash in the summer of 1974. Industrial production in the capitalist world fell by 10 per cent between July 1974 and April 1975. Intra-metropolitan trade fell by 13 per cent. It was far and away the biggest crash since 1929.

Its immediate cause was a collapse of capitalist confidence. Accumulation fell sharply. Private investment in the OECD countries as a whole dropped by 13 per cent between 1973 and 1975. The collapse in investment triggered off a classic downward spiral into slump as realisation difficulties spread.

A number of developments contributed to the collapse of confidence which precipitated the sharp fall in investment. At the political level, the summer of 1974 was the time of Watergate and the near victory of the left in the French presidential elections. Economically, the period was one of major credit failures and near-misses, the most important being the collapse of the giant Herstatt Bank. Seeking to isolate a single triggering factor is probably not a fruitful activity.

Though the precise timing of the crash is hard to explain, the underlying causes are not difficult to locate. The conditions for producing surplus value had been poor since the late 1960s. The mini-boom had shown that even a spectacular improvement in the conditions for realising surplus value did next to nothing to improve those for producing it, and was insufficient to bring about a sustained expansion. Profitability had hardly risen during 1972–73 and investment had not taken off. The oil crisis had aggravated the poor conditions for producing and realising surplus value and the government's cuts in spending and tight money policies had further worsened those for realisation. Capital's collapse of confidence was hardly irrational.

The resulting slump left many factories silent and millions on the dole. By autumn 1975 about 11 per cent of fixed capital was out of use. Unemployment in the metropolitan countries rose from about eight million at the end of the mini-boom to about fifteen million in spring 1975. And this figure is a gross underestimate of jobs lost: participation rates (the proportion of the population officially recorded as in or seeking work) declined sharply, underemployment rose and the number of immigrant workers in Europe fell by over a million.

Profitability took a nose dive as markets contracted, causing more intense competition and pressure on profit margins as the most efficient producers fought to maintain sales by forcing out weaker rivals. The proportion of machines in use fell and overhead costs per unit of output rose.

By winter 1974–75 then, the crisis had assumed the classic form of a slump. After years of increasing inflation and instability, mass unemployment had once more emerged in the metropolitan heartland. It has remained with us ever since.

Crawling stagnation

Developments since 1975

The situation in the metropolitan economies since the bottoming out of the 1974–75 slump is best described as one of crawling

5: a Output, Exports and Prices: Advanced Capitalist World, 1962–79

| | Rate of growth in percentages | | | | |
	Average 1962–73	1973–74	1974–75	1975–76	Average 1976–79
Real output	5	0.25	−1	5	3.5
Volume of exports	8.5	7	−4	10.5	5.5
Consumer prices	4	13.5	10.5	8	7.5

5: b Unemployment: Advanced Capitalist World, 1962–79

| | Percentage of total labour force | | | | |
	1962–73	1974	1975	1976	1977–79
Unemployment	3	3.5	5.5	5.5	5.25

Source: Midland Bank Review, *February 1978; OECD,* Economic Outlook, *July 1979.*

stagnation. There has not yet been another crash. But the short burst of fairly rapid growth which took place in 1976 could not be sustained. By 1979, production in the capitalist world was 18 per cent below the level it would have been had it held the growth rate of the years 1963–73. Unemployment has hovered around a level ten million or so above that of the sixties, and prices have continued to rise at a rate of 7 or 8 per cent a year. These developments are summarised in Table 5 opposite.

The OECD had already forecast a further slowdown in growth and acceleration of prices before OPEC announced another sharp oil price increase in June 1979. After that news, it suggested that a 2 per cent growth in output and a 9 per cent inflation rate were optimistic predictions for 1980.

The immediate cause of the stagnation of output was the sluggishness of accumulation. Investment fell by 13 per cent in the capitalist world during 1974 and 1975 and by 1978 was still below the 1973 peak in France, Italy and Japan – the economies in which accumulation had been most rapid in the years immediately preceding 1973 (see Table 6 below). In total, it was only three-quarters of what it would have been if pre-1973 trends had been maintained.

6: Private Business Investment

	France	Italy	West Germany	Japan	UK	US
Indices (1973 = 100)						
1975	91	88	88	78	94	84
1978	95	95	107	88	111	103

Source: OECD, Economic Outlook, *July 1977, 1978, 1979.*

Investment did begin to rise quite sharply during 1978, especially in W. Germany. This was because the rate of accumulation had fallen so much that even the slow growth of output achieved meant that plant which could be operated profitably at existing wage and price levels was in short supply.

But the OECD's survey for July 1979 argued that investment was likely to fall off again quickly, since capital expected higher-priced materials to squeeze profits further. Although profitability has risen somewhat since 1975, it has not at the time of writing, regained even the inadequate level of 1973 in any major country, except the US.

More than half a decade of stagnation has also proved insufficient to bring inflation down to pre-1974 levels. The rate at which prices have risen has fallen below the peak reached in the wake of the oil crisis, but has stubbornly remained within the 7–8 per cent range. And the recent round of oil price rises threatens renewed acceleration.

A lengthy period of poor conditions for realisation has had such a limited effect on inflation primarily because of workers' success in resisting cuts in living standards. Despite high levels of unemployment, the working class has remained able to win fairly substantial increases in money wages, which it has regarded as essential to offset the price rises it has come to expect. With productivity growth slow as a result of the low rate of accumulation – it has averaged around 3 per cent a year in the capitalist world since 1975 as opposed to a previous rate of some 4 per cent – capital has sought to protect profits by passing on increased wage costs in higher prices. Governments have so far been willing to accommodate these price rises by operating mildly expansionary monetary and fiscal policies.

Why has stagnation persisted?

Renewed accumulation would require an improvement in both the conditions for producing surplus value and those for realising it. Capitalists will not undertake substantial productive investment unless they can produce additional goods profitably and sell them. This has not been possible since the onset of slump in 1974.

The conditions for producing and realising surplus value are generally bad in a slump. Markets are comparatively stagnant and profitability is adversely affected because the large number of idle machines raises unit costs. This is true regardless of the situation prior to the slump.

In the present situation, however, the difficulties are compounded by the fact that a marked deterioration in the conditions for producing surplus value began in the 1960s, well before the onset of slump, in contrast to the situation in the 1930s, which was not preceded by a general decline in profitability.

The second fundamental feature of the present situation is the strength of the organised working class. This strength makes the fall in profitability all the more serious, because attempts to increase potential surplus value through wage cuts, higher work intensity and other such measures are likely to be opposed.

The metropolitan working class entered the present crisis stronger in trade union terms than ever before. And that strength has not been broken to date. This is in sharp contrast to the thirties, when crisis came after major defeats, including the General Strike in the UK and the victory of fascism in Italy. Further defeats occurred during the crisis. The most powerful national organisations in working-class history were destroyed within months of the Nazi seizure of power in Germany.

The fundamental problem for capital

Accumulation always proceeds along a tightrope. Consider wages. If accumulation is to continue smoothly, real wages must develop within a certain band. They must not rise so rapidly that conditions for producing surplus value deteriorate enough to prevent capitalists from accumulating further. Nor must they grow so slowly that the conditions for realisation are adversely affected. The parameters of this band will depend on specific historical circumstances.

Once the system has toppled off the tightrope and slump sets in the conditions for both producing and realising surplus value are poor. Capital as a whole faces the following problem. Developments which would improve the conditions for producing surplus value tend to worsen those for realising it. Conversely, developments which would improve the conditions for realising surplus value tend simultaneously to worsen those for producing it.

To return to wages, increases in their real value would improve the conditions for realisation. Demand for consumer goods would go up, thus expanding markets and stimulating capitalists to invest. But such an increase would have an adverse effect on the conditions for producing surplus value. It would increase wage costs, tending to reduce potential surplus value. A fall in real wages clearly has equally contradictory effects.

The response of capital

Despite this catch-22 situation for the system as a whole, a rise in wage costs is unambiguously bad for an individual firm. The conditions for producing surplus value deteriorate and those for realising it do not improve. It increases costs but, since expenditure by the firm's own workforce is a negligible proportion of total expenditure on its products, does not expand markets. Similarly, a fall in wage costs improves the conditions for producing surplus value without worsening those for realising it.

The response of individual capitalists to the onset of slump is therefore predictable. They will intensify efforts to reduce costs by holding down wages, 'shaking out' labour, imposing speed-up and so on. In other words, capitalists as controllers of units of capital will concentrate exclusively on improving conditions for producing surplus value.

This response is rational in that it offers a possible solution for individual capitals. If a firm can reduce unit costs by more than its competitors, it can raise profitability while simultaneously reducing prices relative to those charged by rivals, thereby expanding sales at their expense.

However, if capitalists as a whole manage to drive down wage costs relative to prices, they reduce the volume of consumer goods that can be sold. The conditions for realisation deteriorate and stagnation intensifies. Successful attempts by individual capitalists to solve one problem exacerbate the other.

Options open to the state

State policies also influence developments. Demand-management (i.e. manipulation of government spending, taxation and credit) enables the state to exert considerable influence on the conditions for realisation. If the government increases its expenditure, for example, this gives markets a boost.

If potential surplus value were adequate, this 'pump priming' would stimulate capital to increase investment. This increase in investment would further expand markets for capitalists producing means of production, who would take on more workers. Consumer demand would go up and expand markets still more. The process would become self-sustaining – at least for a while.

Since demand management policies influence employment (via the conditions for realisation), they also provide the state with a tool for shaping the conditions under which surplus value is produced. The effect of contractionary policies, such as a reduction in state spending, is to raise unemployment, weaken the working class – making it easier to hold down real wages and drive up productivity – and thus help capital to re-establish an adequate rate of potential surplus value.

Demand-management can be used to improve either the conditions for realising surplus value or those for producing it. But what if both are inadequate? The problem, from the point of view of the authorities, is that diametrically opposed measures are required to improve these two sets of conditions.

The response of governments

The response available to an individual unit of capital is also open to a national-capitalist economy. The world market – recreated during the long boom – allows surplus value produced in one economy to be realised in another. Commodities can be exported rather than sold on the home market. If a national economy can cut costs by more than its international competitors, it can simultaneously raise profits, cut prices relative to its rivals and solve realisation problems by expanding its share of world trade.

To the extent that states are committees for managing the common affairs of their national ruling classes, it therefore makes sense for them to implement policies which will assist their capitals' attempts to reduce costs.

Governments understand that relative costs must be reduced if sales are to expand in the context of stagnant world markets. This explains their unwillingness to undertake unilateral reflation on a scale sufficient to reduce unemployment. They realise that an expansion would reduce capital's chances of improving international competitiveness. **This appreci**ation also lies behind talk of export-led booms – fanciful predictions that the conditions for realising surplus value abroad will improve as a country gains a larger share of world markets – which serve as a 'justification' for not expanding the domestic economy significantly.

The adverse impact of unilateral reflation on international competitiveness cannot fully explain the clearly observable reluctance of governments to undertake internationally coordinated expansion. If all national economies reflated equally, none would lose competitive advantage and markets would grow overall. So why do they not do it?

One reason is that each hopes to gain a competitive advantage by expanding later and by less than the others, thereby winning an increased share of world markets. So long as total surplus value is inadequate, the major powers cannot agree how to share it out between them. But, even if they did overcome this problem, there would still be a more fundamental one. Expansion would reduce unemployment and strengthen the working class internationally.

The immediate effects of internationally coordinated expansion would favour capital. Better conditions for realisation would enable sales and production to go up. Profit margins would rise because more goods would be produced, and so overhead costs would be spread over a larger number of units. Better realisation conditions would also mean prices could go up, which would raise profit margins further.

The problem from capital's viewpoint is that the working class would be unlikely to resign itself to a higher cost of living. And the fall in unemployment would strengthen its ability to resist. The initial gain in profitability would rapidly be wiped out by wage increases. Capital would find itself without better conditions for producing surplus value, and a stronger working class would make future improvement even harder to achieve.

Further expansion would mean another round of price increases, but workers would respond as before, so that expansion could well set off a wage/price spiral – to use conventional economic journalese. The authorities would hardly relish the prospect of clashes over rising prices while the working class was relatively strong because of high demand for labour.

The end of the road?

The world capitalist system has been characterised by stagnation, punctuated by only the feeblest of upswings, for the last six years. The problems are intractable. Capital has been having real trouble dealing with a combination of low profitability, stagnant markets and a strong working class.

And four developments have intensified capital's difficulties during the years of stagnation. The first is that imperialism has weakened on a world scale, as illustrated by the defeat of the US in South East Asia and the Shah of Iran's involuntary exit.

Mounting political instability in 'peripheral' countries restricts metropolitan capital's room for manoeuvre. It makes investment in such countries decreasingly attractive, thus hindering one potential way of improving conditions for producing surplus value: relocation in low-wage countries. It threatens export markets, which are important for realisation. It threatens previously reliable and cheap sources of materials and fuel, which makes the restoring of adequate conditions for producing surplus value in the metropoles more difficult. The capitalist press anticipates each meeting of OPEC with impotent horror. Confident predictions in 1974 that the price of oil would collapse as soon as growth slackened seem foolish now.

Second, capital's problems have been intensified by the decreasing stability in trade relations between advanced capitalist economies. Governments are tempted to try and secure an advantage by declaring they will not accept competitor nations' products while seeking to continue peddling their own abroad – so-called protectionism. Many commentators have expressed disquiet about this development. For example, the General Agreement on Tariffs and Trade Report for 1977 pointed to 'a worldwide and disturbing resurgence of protectionist pressure which in recent months has reached a level not experienced for more than a generation' (p.7).

An individual national-capitalist economy can expand its share of world markets either by increasing exports or reducing imports. What matters, in terms of realisation, is the relative rates of growth of the two. Raising the rate of potential surplus value, while reducing imports relative to exports, therefore represents a possible way out of the dilemma faced by individual economies.

If economies in particularly acute difficulties introduced major protectionist measures, this could well spark off a chain reaction, with world trade collapsing as a result. The effect would be to depress accumulation even further, as capital found itself increasingly limited by the confines of the home market.

The third development which has increased the vulnerability of the system is a decline in financial stability. One aspect of this process has been an enormous growth in indebtedness within advanced countries, especially the US. Low profitability has forced firms further into debt. Consumer borrowing has also continued to grow; outstanding debt is now 80 per cent of disposable income, one-tenth higher than in 1974. This growth has made both capital and workers' expenditure more vulnerable to a major credit squeeze.

Peripheral countries have also acquired huge debts in the wake of the oil crisis. Brazil, Mexico, Venezuela, Hong Kong and Singapore have each borrowed more than $10 billion from international banks. *Euromoney* magazine reported in April 1979 that the 'average' third world country now has an external debt of 29 per cent of annual output and debt servicing (interest and scheduled loan repayments) represents 16 per cent of exports. A typically 'vulnerable' country has a balance of payments deficit of 13 per cent of output, external debt of 59 per cent of annual production, and debt servicing of 41 per cent of exports. The 1979 round of oil price increases is expected to push the combined deficit of the 'non-oil' peripheral countries to $50 billion in 1980. The chances of a really major default are high.

But the most serious aspect of financial instability is the increased vulnerability of the dollar. Dollar holdings by foreigners have continued to grow apace. By April 1979, foreign central banks held $141 billion as reserves and foreign capitalists about half that figure. Dollars held abroad in the Euro-dollar market now total well over $300 billion. American corporations hold billions of dollars surplus to their expenditure needs in the US. They could provoke a major financial crisis by switching a small proportion of these funds into other currencies.

Finally, capital's control over economic activity has been

increasingly threatened of late by mass workers' parties adopting left programmes, including proposals for investment controls and nationalisation. Parties committed to such programmes are, or have recently been, an immediately pressing problem for capital in Britain, Italy, France and Spain.

This last development serves as a timely reminder of the real nature of capital's difficulties. These cannot be explained by claiming supplies of labour have run out. Even if every able-bodied human being in the capitalist world were in waged employment, this would in itself constrain only the maximum rate of accumulation consistent with a particular set of production techniques. It would not mean inevitable unemployment, stagnation or crisis.

Of course labour reserves have not been completely drained. The supply of labour is largely socially determined, as is plain enough from the post-war importance of such factors as immigration and the proportion of women in waged work. Production techniques used are similarly subject to social determination, being shaped by capitalists' expectations concerning factors such as real wages and input costs.

Crisis is not a result of circumstances which render continued full employment and growth physically impossible. It has occurred because the system is unable to adjust smoothly to changed circumstances. The problems are economic and political rather than physical. It is capitalism, and not nature, that is to blame.

2.
The Decline of UK Competitiveness

Competitiveness, Productivity and Accumulation

Economic developments in the UK during the seventies were dominated by British capital's astonishingly rapid decline in ability to compete in international markets. The decline had begun almost a century earlier and gathered momentum in the nineteen-fifties and sixties. But its pace, importance and seeming inevitability were all magnified in the seventies.

Competitiveness is an inherently relative notion. It has meaning only in comparison with the performance of rivals. Other things being equal, the more rapid the development of other economies, the more rapid the decline in UK competitiveness. In this sense, the phenomenal economic success of Europe and Japan during the long boom can be seen as a prime cause of the UK's decline.

But the boom also postponed and temporarily mitigated the effects of decline. It did so in two ways. Firstly, by ensuring a large pool of world surplus value, it reduced the intensity of struggle between national capitals over its division. So long as the stronger powers had plenty, they were unwilling to rock the international boat by squeezing the UK too hard.

Secondly, world markets were expanding rapidly, which tempered the fact that the UK's share was shrinking. So long as the total grew, a falling share did not necessarily mean an absolute fall. While the boom lasted, the UK was able to secure markets for an increasing volume of output despite declining competitiveness.

It did not feel the full effects of declining competitiveness until the onset of crisis in the seventies. Once world surplus value fell and markets stagnated, the struggle over market division intensified. Falling shares became incompatible with absolute increases, and UK capital had to face immediate, severe difficulties.

The policy responses to these problems are the subject of the next two chapters. This one looks at their roots in the fifties and sixties.

Productivity in the UK: comparative and historical

The best historical data available on comparative rates of growth of industrial productivity is reproduced in Table 1 below.

1: Rate of Growth of Industrial Productivity

	Average annual percentages		
	1889–1913	1913–1938	1938–1968
UK	0.4	1.1	1.6
US	1.4	1.7	3.0
W. Germany	2.1	1.2	2.2
Italy		1.4	3.5
Japan		3.8	2.6

Source: Phelps-Brown, Table 3 (US 1913–37, 1937–68); G. Fua, Table 1.9; K. Ohkawa and H. Rosovsky, BST 4, 14, 15.

In the two and a half decades immediately before the first world war, UK productivity growth was pitifully slow in comparison to that achieved by its major competitors. By 1913, the level of UK productivity was about half that of the US and barely above that of Germany.

There was some improvement after that. Between 1913 and 1938, productivity grew almost as rapidly in the UK as in its major European competitors (probably including France), although more slowly than in the US. The productivity of Japanese industry rose spectacularly from an initially low level.

The period from the second world war onwards was disastrous for UK capital, which failed to match the rate of productivity growth achieved by any of its major competitors. In the US productivity rose substantially during the war to a position of overwhelming superiority which was maintained for the next 20 years. German and French productivity was slow to recover from the war, but then surged ahead. Even Italy and Japan, which had hardly rated as serious industrial powers before the war, achieved UK levels of productivity in leading industries by the late 1960s.

The period of poor performance prior to the first world war did not have immediately disastrous consequences for UK competitiveness because British capital still enjoyed a higher level of productivity than most of its competitors. This was no longer the case by the end of the post-war period. By 1970, UK industrial productivity was approximately one-third of the US level, two-thirds of that of France, W. Germany and the smaller Northern European economies and about the same as the Italian level. Slow productivity growth had more immediately damaging effects in this later period, because the proportion of goods traded internationally was higher than that at the turn of the century and because the UK had fallen back from the position of pack leader to that of laggard.

Accumulation and productivity

Marxists have traditionally argued that the rate of capital accumulation is the main determinant of the long-run rate of growth of productivity, because it is primarily through accumulation that the labour process incorporates changes in technique. This thesis is supported by data which have recently been assembled for the major capitalist economies over the last century. (see Table 2 opposite).

There is a very close association between the rate of increase of the mass of fixed capital per worker (technical composition of capital) and that of productivity. Over the last hundred years the rate of accumulation per head and productivity growth in the UK have lagged behind those of major competitors by between $\frac{3}{4}$ per cent to $1\frac{1}{2}$ per cent a year.

The low rate of accumulation in the UK during the long boom was unquestionably a major cause of the slow growth in productivity over that period. Why was it so low?

2: Accumulation and Productivity: Whole Economy 1870–1970

	Average annual percentages	
	Rate of growth of stock of capital per worker	Rate of growth of hourly labour productivity
France (1913–1970)	2.6	2.8
W. Germany	1.9	2.4
Italy (1882–1970)	2.5	2.5
Japan (1880–1970)	2.7	2.9
UK	1.0	1.6
US	1.8	2.3

Source: Maddison 1979, pp. 19, 41, 43.

The post-war inheritance: reality and myth

Victory and defeat

The countries which did best during the fifties and sixties were those which suffered defeat in the war. (Table 3: note that while France finished up on the winning side it was, nevertheless, a defeated power). This outcome appears perverse.

The UK emerged from the war a victor. Its economy was physically relatively undamaged during the hostilities and functioning effectively, with most available machinery put to use. It had no large influx of refugees to support. Its empire was more or less intact. A Labour government, dominated by a right-wing leadership, contained pressures towards mass radicalisation within fairly safe parliamentary channels.

Contrast this situation with that of the defeated powers. Japan is the extreme example. Economic dislocation was severe, with production running at only a fraction of pre-war levels. The empire was dismembered and millions of refugees required support. The working class moved rapidly leftwards in the context of extreme economic hardship and the political vacuum left by discredited traditional leaders.

Yet Japan, Germany and at times Italy, were the great post-war success stories for the ruling class. The UK was a loser.

Paradoxically, much of the explanation for the UK's poor post-war performance lies in its seemingly enviable, smooth transition from war to peace. So the analysis below concentrates on the first decade or so after the war.

3: Capital and Productivity: Industry, 1953–72

	Average annual percentages	
	Rate of growth of capital stock	Rate of growth of productivity
France	5.8	5.4
W. Germany	7.0	5.0
Italy	6.6	5.0
Japan	12.5	8.9
UK	4.2	3.0
US	3.3	2.7

Source: Boltho, Tables 1.1 and 1.2.

War damage

It is often argued that wartime destruction benefited the defeated powers by wiping out old means of production and thereby 'clearing the way' for investment in new ones. That this proposition can be put forward at all is a fine illustration of the absurd contradictions characterising capitalism. In a socialist system it would be self-evident that the destruction of a proportion of existing means of production could have only negative economic effects.

In any case, the argument does not hold up. In Japan, which experienced the greatest destruction, capital stock had regained the pre-war level by about 1950, since the extensive damage was in large part offset by feverish wartime accumulation. A survey of war damage in the W. German engineering industry, which exceeded that elsewhere in Europe, concluded that it was hardly significant in relation to capacity. At the end of the war, capacity in W. Germany far exceeded that at the beginning. The collapse of production in the defeated powers was due less to lost capacity than to shortages of materials and transport, and to social, economic and political disorganisation. So it is nonsense to argue that post-war investment in the UK was low because little of its productive capacity was destroyed by bombing.

Controls, competition and bad management

But other legacies from the war years did perpetuate a low rate of accumulation in the UK. The forces of competition, which had not been strong for some time, were weakened further. Wartime controls included price-fixing intended to ensure 'reasonable' profits for low efficiency producers, making aggressive pricing impossible. Physical quotas for materials and investment goods more or less froze market shares and prevented energetic investment programmes.

The controls were in many cases administered by leading capitalists from the industries concerned. Unilever had 90 employees seconded to the Ministry of Food, for example, and the Match Industry Controller not only worked for Bryant and May, but also had his office on company premises. These are not isolated examples.

Harold Wilson, then President of the Board of Trade, later described the system as one which:

> perpetuates the pattern of a particular industry or trade, feather-beds the inefficient and unenterprising, freezes out the newcomers and penalises the efficient growing firm. It has, in fact, many of the vices of the old pre-war type of control [i.e. cartels] dividing out whole markets on the basis of arbitrary quotas, and doing this with all the statutory sanction of the state behind it. (*Future* 1 January 1954).

Competitive pressure remained fairly stifled even after formal controls were removed in the late forties and early fifties. The Restrictive Practices Court reported that by 1961 2,350 restrictive practices were registered with them while 1,250 had been abandoned (at least officially), probably in order to avoid investigation by the Court. Co-operation rather than cut-throat competition had become a way of life for many companies.

This situation was in stark contrast with that in the defeated powers. Pre-war Japan is often cited as a prime example of an economy lacking competition, with control concentrated in the hands of a few giant *zaibatsu* (literally 'money clique') groups. This concentration was real and little affected by the official break-up of the groups by the US occupation authorities after the war. But it did not mean there was no competition.

Competition is not a matter of numbers. Two giant companies may compete in a thoroughly cut-throat manner, while another industry may contain many small firms which do not act aggressively towards each other. The *zaibatsu* competed fiercely in a wide range of markets.

What effect did the lack of vigorous competition in the UK have on accumulation? It is not possible to quantify, but is likely to have been considerable.

The best evidence available suggests that profits in the UK were not lower than elsewhere in the early years of the boom. But UK capital invested a smaller proportion of profits than did its foreign rivals (Table 4 below).

4: Profits and Investment as a Proportion of Manufacturing Output 1951–55

	Average annual percentages	
	Profits	Investment
UK	34	11
US	29	11
Italy	28	22
W. Germany	38	18
Japan	32	20

Source: Armstrong et al. Table 10.

It would have been surprising if controls of the type in operation in the UK had not reduced accumulation. In such a system – in effect a single, state-backed cartel for each industry –

capitalists can be expected to undertake replacement investment and to add small pieces of plant to meet anticipated market growth. But there is neither incentive nor pressure to undertake major investments in new techniques, which often require a substantial increase in market share if they are to pay off.

Finally, the popular notion that poor UK performance is a product of bad management probably derives from the absence of an aggressive competitive structure. Plants of UK multi-nationals located abroad, and staffed by British management teams, did notably better than their counterparts at home. A lack of cut-throat competition breeds bad managers rather than the other way round.

Competition in external markets

The contrast between the UK and the defeated powers in the extent of competitive pressure on capital is even sharper in the sphere of export markets.

About half of all UK exports went to the Sterling Area (a group of ex-colonies which used sterling for international payments and kept their reserves in London). A system of preferential tariffs protected UK sales in these markets from foreign competition. The Sterling Area was in effect treated as an extension of the domestic market.

Japanese capital fared rather differently. Its protected imperial markets (the inappropriately named Greater South-East Asia Co-Prosperity Sphere) disappeared. About 40 per cent of pre-war exports were lost as a result. A further 10 per cent fell victim to the collapse of the silk trade when nylon arrived. Perhaps 20 per cent more were displaced by the development of indigenous textile industries. All in all, little remained.

The need to expand exports to pay for essential imports was pressing. Extensive modernisation programmes were rapidly carried out, in part through government intervention, in the steel and chemicals sectors. These were the most likely candidates for future export successes, although not at the time internationally competitive. The need to break into new markets abroad thus stimulated accumulation in Japan.

Foreign investment

British capital had traditionally invested abroad on a massive scale. In the decade immediately before the first world war, for example, foreign investment not only absorbed 7 per cent of national income, but also exceeded investment in the UK. But did investment abroad inhibit domestic accumulation in the postwar period, as is often alleged?

Foreign investment could in principle reduce that at home by starving potential domestic investors of funds. But there is no evidence that this occurred in the fifties. As argued below, UK capital was not bound by financing constraints at that time.

So the argument that foreign investment seriously inhibited domestic accumulation is hard to sustain. In the fifties, direct investment abroad (the building of plant overseas, as opposed to the purchase of foreign stocks and shares, 'portfolio' investment) was only 13 per cent of investment in the UK, and absorbed less than half the earnings from earlier investment overseas.

It is also wrong to assume a pre-given total volume of investment (determined by market growth, say) and hence to conclude that domestic investment must have been reduced whenever investment abroad was increased. Particular projects were undoubtedly 'diverted' abroad, but they probably account for only a small proportion of foreign investment.

Finally, even if British capital did turn overseas, this was largely because it was difficult to produce competitively for export from the UK. Capital's attitude was more a result of the domestic situation than an explanation for it.

Sterling

Another imperial heritage was the role of sterling as an international currency (one held along with the dollar in foreign exchange reserves). It is widely argued that the maintenance of this role for sterling was a victory for banking over industrial capital and contributed to the poor post-war performance of the latter.

It is certainly true that the City of London regarded sterling's world status as a necessary foundation for its international financial operations and fought hard to maintain the pound's role.

As a consequence, the UK became more vulnerable to balance of payments problems. Deficits on external balance could be magnified by speculative runs on the pound. These became frequent and on occasion prompted the government to take deflationary action, cutting demand to reduce imports and raising interest rates to persuade foreigners to continue holding sterling. (Under capitalism even 'confidence' has its price.)

Deflation to protect the balance of payments constituted the 'stop' phase of the notorious 'stop-go' cycle of the fifties and early sixties. Some commentators believe this cycle seriously inhibited accumulation since capitalists correctly surmised that upswings ('go' phases) would not continue long enough to justify substantial investment. But the argument is problematic.

Japanese capital – to continue our extended comparison – also experienced a series of 'stops' in the fifties and early sixties, prompted by balance of payments difficulties. But the strong upward surge of accumulation continued in spite of this stumbling. Japanese capitalists just paused for breath and then continued with massive investment programmes.

There is no evidence that UK cycles bit deeper than Japanese ones. Yet British capitalists held back from investing while their Japanese rivals strained at the leash.

A related effect of sterling's international role was the City's resistance to devaluation, which it believed (wrongly as it turned out) would damage its position as an international financial centre. This resistance certainly delayed the devaluation which eventually occurred in 1967 and which, it is often argued, was badly needed by industrial capital to help offset the negative effect of slow productivity growth on competitiveness.

But the benefits of devaluation are often exaggerated. A permanent improvement is possible only if industrial capital takes advantage of the temporary easing of international competitive pressure to undertake a major modernisation drive. This did not happen in 1967.

Without modernisation, the benefits of devaluation tend to be eroded rapidly as workers wrest larger wage increases to offset the rise in living costs caused by higher import prices. The events of the late sixties and seventies have shown clearly that devaluation is not in itself a panacea for an uncompetitive economy. It seems likely that one of the most important effects of postponing devaluation was a corresponding postponement of sharper inflation in its wake (see below).

It is thus difficult to sustain the argument that the role of sterling was a major cause of poor UK performance. The overvalued exchange rate and consequent 'stop/go' cycles at most exacerbated other, more deep-rooted problems.

Defence spending

The defeated powers were initially forbidden to re-arm. But the British ruling class was obliged, both by its own conception of its world role and by pressure from the US, to maintain a high level of defence expenditure. At its peak in 1952, defence accounted for 9.8 per cent of output. By 1968 it still accounted for more than 5 per cent.

Defence spending set a clear physical limit to industrial investment in the late forties and early fifties, when controls were used to divert scarce engineering capacity to armaments production. More generally, since defence expenditure absorbs surplus value, it reduces the proportion potentially available for accumulation.

But, although defence spending limited investment *possibilities* in this way, it is not clear that it held down the *actual* level of investment. There is little evidence that capitalists wished to accumulate more surplus value than was available to them.

When defence-related controls were relaxed after 1952, there was no great upsurge in investment. Nor was there an upsurge in inflation, such as would have resulted from capitalists competing for scarce investable resources. This was not due to financing constraints. Between 1952 and 1956, UK non-financial companies spent only about two-thirds of the profits that they retained on new equipment.

A high level of defence expenditure may, however, have held down the level of desired investment. There are a number of possible mechanisms, of which taxation is probably the most important. Defence contributed to the government's revenue requirements, part of which were covered by taxing capital. At least half of company profits were taken in taxes in the fifties. This did not actively constrain financing, but may have reduced the incentive to invest.

The defence burden may also have inhibited accumulation by channelling research and development (R and D) effort into avenues of military rather than commercial value. A higher proportion of national income was devoted to R and D in the UK than in other major countries in the early sixties. But 40 per cent of such expenditure was in the military and space fields, compared to 15 per cent in W. Germany.

This emphasis led to a heavy concentration of R and D in the aircraft industry. UK companies spent as high a proportion of revenue on R and D as did the American giants. But the US companies were so much bigger that the UK's attempt to keep up was an expensive folly born of imperial delusions.

R and D expenditure was low in international comparative terms in more commercially crucial sectors. In machinery, UK companies spent only one-third the proportion of sales revenue that their US counterparts devoted to R and D. In the early sixties, the UK devoted only 46 per cent of R and D expenditure to the vital vehicles, machinery and chemical sectors as compared to Japan's 69 per cent and W. Germany's 86 per cent.

It is, of course, not necessarily the case that any R and D resources released from defence would have been employed elsewhere. Many sectors of mechanical engineering scarcely had any graduate engineers in R and D (or, indeed, any other function) before the 1960s.

The role of defence expenditure in limiting the rate and effectiveness of accumulation is difficult to assess. It certainly imposed limits on the rate, but it is far from clear that UK capital ever wished to invest up to these limits. However, the high levels of corporation tax, imposed partly because of the need to finance defence spending, may have contributed to capital's lack of desire to invest.

The 1945–51 Labour government

Another particularly important respect in which the transition from war to boom was unfavourable for British capital concerns relations between capital and labour. These generally receive little

attention in left-wing discussions of the post-war decline of the UK
– a major weakness of them.

The British ruling class appeared to have achieved a
remarkably smooth transition from the widespread demands
for radical social change which characterised the close of hostilities to the 13 years of Tory rule which began in 1951. The bridge
between the two periods was, of course, the 1945–51 Labour
government.

Labour mobilised working-class radicalisation behind a left-
wing programme which included:

- public ownership of fuel and power, inland transport and iron
  and steel;
- public supervision and control of monopolies;
- domestic policies of planning, 'keeping a firm constructive
  hand on the whole productive machinery'.

But, once in office, Labour did little to threaten capital. On
the contrary, its policies became anti-working-class. Major
nationalisation proposals were indeed implemented. But the
manner chosen was perfectly acceptable to the majority of the
capitalist class, which recognised the need for reorganisation in the
industries concerned. No real elements of workers' control or
management were introduced. The commitment to planning was
abandoned. Wartime controls were dismantled as soon as practicable and central planning was denounced in 1948 as intrinsically
undemocratic. Wage controls held the rate of growth of real
consumption per head down to $\frac{1}{2}$ per cent a year after 1947. Anti-
strike legislation dating from the war was used against workers.
Labour thus diluted mass radicalisation and paved the way for the
Tories.

This relatively painless process contrasts sharply with major
class confrontations in the defeated powers. In Japan, for
example, the immediate post-war years saw a massive wave of
unionisation sweep through industry. 'Production control', a
system whereby workers occupied factories and operated them in
conjunction with other plants, was widespread. Workers took
over a leading Tokyo newspaper and promptly sacked the arch-
reactionary editor. Local committees, organising food distribution and the like, represented embryonic workers' councils. The

ruling class was incapable of governing effectively even with the support of the US occupation authorities.

Though the British ruling class had a relatively easy time maintaining control, accounts which consider only the advantages of the smooth transition are misleading.

The welfare state

One possible disadvantage to the ruling class of the 1945–51 Labour government which is sometimes mentioned is the creation of the welfare state. Some commentators argue that the creation of the National Health Service, the improvement of social insurance and so on played a role similar to that of defence expenditure. They say it impeded accumulation by diverting resources that would otherwise have been available for investment. The argument is unconvincing.

Contrary to popular belief, the proportion of national income devoted to government civil expenditure in the UK in the early 1950s was some 5 per cent lower than in continental Europe (see Table 5 below).

5: Government Expenditure as a Proportion of Total Output, 1952–56

| | Average annual percentages | |
	Military expenditure	Current civil expenditure (including transfers)
UK	8.3	15.0
France	6.3	20.8
W. Germany	3.8	21.6
Italy	3.9	20.5
Japan	14.1	

Source: OECD, National Accounts 1950–68.

As with defence, government civil spending certainly sets limits to the maximum possible rate of accumulation. But it is far from clear that UK capital ever wished to accumulate beyond these limits. Had it attempted to do so, there would almost certainly have been inflation as capital competed with other sectors for resources. In fact, prices rose only gently until the mid-1960s.

The real importance of UK working-class strength for government spending and capital accumulation lies not in the volume of state spending, but in who paid for it.

Pressure from the labour movement ensured that much government spending was financed by taxing capital. The pre-tax share of profits in national income rose from 12 to 14 per cent between 1938 and 1951, but the post-tax share fell from 9 to 5 per cent. Capital as a whole was unable to 'pass on' taxes as higher prices during this period because the development of pre-tax real wages was largely determined, independently of tax burdens and money-wage bargaining, by the requirements of accumulation (see below).

Since, as argued above, capital faced no effective financing constraints, the high tax burden did not ultimately limit investment possibilities. But it may well have reduced the incentive to accumulate.

Labour shortage

A crucial aspect of the balance of power between labour and capital is the existence of relatively full employment in the UK until the mid-sixties. Demobilisation did not lead to widespread unemployment. By 1950, registered unemployment had fallen to a level barely above 1 per cent of the labour force and only small and temporary increases were recorded over the next 15 years.

The level of registered unemployment in the UK is a more reliable indicator of the reserves of labour available to capital than it is in the case of Europe and Japan, which had large reserves of under-employed workers in agriculture, on which capital could draw. The UK possessed no such reserves. Capital here faced a labour shortage.

This meant that real (pre-tax) wages rose. The mechanism was the process of 'scrapping' outlined in Chapter 1. As capital accumulated, more workers were required to operate newly installed machines. To the extent that the rate at which new machines were installed exceeded that at which the labour force grew, the new machines could be equipped with operators only if enough of their older counterparts were withdrawn from use. Old machines would be scrapped only when wages rose enough to render their continued use unprofitable. The greater the rate of accumulation, therefore, the more rapid the rise in real wages.

The modest rate of accumulation achieved by UK capital immediately after the war was sufficient to ensure that real wages rose more or less in line with productivity. During the fifties and early sixties, wages rose slightly more rapidly than productivity and the share of company output appropriated as pre-tax profit declined from about 25 per cent in the mid-fifties to around 20 per cent in the mid-sixties. This indicates that the low rate of accumulation nevertheless exceeded that which the economy could sustain in the context of labour shortage.

The fundamental problem was the slow increase in the technical composition of capital which meant that the demand for labour was too high and the rate of productivity growth too low. If only accumulation had proceeded on the basis of a more rapid growth in the amount of equipment per worker then a higher rate could have been sustained and a more rapid growth of productivity achieved without the need for accelerated scrapping. Competitiveness could have been maintained without profits being squeezed.

France and W. Germany enjoyed considerably higher rates of accumulation in the fifties and sixties than did the UK. But their rates of employment growth were not correspondingly higher. This was because of the form of investment they undertook. French and German capitalists invested in techniques involving a considerably more rapid increase in the technical composition than those their UK rivals chose.

Conventional economic theory would regard this pattern as perverse. It would argue that a shortage of labour in the UK should have encouraged increased mechanisation by making labour expensive relative to fixed capital. Wages were indeed higher in the UK than in France or W. Germany in the early fifties. So why did UK capital not mechanise more rapidly?

A number of factors appear to have inhibited mechanisation. Two related ones are the low rate of accumulation and the lack of an aggressive competitive environment. A low rate of investment, geared to maintaining a constant share of a slowly growing market, tends to involve small-scale additions to existing plant. If a productive structure is dominated by old vintages of machine, this tends to inhibit the integration of radically innovative techniques. In contrast, large-scale investment, intended to undercut competitors and increase market shares, tends to involve wholesale incorporation of modern technological developments in 'greenfield' plants built from scratch on new sites. Step-by-step defensive investment involves smaller increases in the technical composition of capital than aggressive 'greenfield' accumulation.

A further factor depressing the level of investment and restricting its form was the strength of working class organisation at factory level. In spite of the policies of the Labour government and the right-wing trade union leadership, shop floor organisation not only remained intact in the early fifties, but was strengthened by a decade of full employment.

The British labour movement was not subjected to anything remotely comparable to the onslaught launched by capital, with help from the US, against its counterparts in Japan and Western Europe. In Japan, for example, public-sector strikes were banned, thousands of Communist Party militants purged and about $\frac{3}{4}$m workers 'rationalised' out of employment. Workers' organisations were smashed through extended lock-outs and replaced by company unions. The phenomenal post-war success of Datsun, to take one example, depended on capital smashing a powerful shop floor organisation after a 100-day strike in 1953.

The UK working class's strong organisation at factory level thwarted many of capital's attempts to increase productivity. New techniques, involving a sharp increase in the technical composition of capital, were often effectively vetoed by unions which did not want to lose jobs. Where new technology was installed, its effect on productivity was often reduced because unions insisted on maintaining existing operating levels or line speeds. Successful resistance of this sort seems the principal explanation for productivity in the post-war UK growing less than three-quarters as fast as the technical composition, whereas the two grew at an approximately equal rate in other countries.

Blaming the workers

To argue that shop floor strength impeded productivity growth is in no sense to accept the ruling class argument that workers are to blame for the crisis. The competitive, class nature of capitalism as a system guarantees that unless workers object, capitalists will introduce changes in the labour process irrespective of their effects on employment, job conditions and so forth. Shop floor action is often the only way workers can protect themselves against the adverse effects of new technology. It is also only because of the competitive nature of capitalism that the adverse effect successful worker resistance sometimes has on productivity growth can provoke crisis, rather than just slower growth in living standards.

Some trade-off between working conditions and living standards is inevitable in any social system. Under socialism, the balance can be consciously and democratically decided. The problem under capitalism is that the trade-off is a side-effect of the interaction of numerous developments, including class struggles, and in certain forms can provoke crises.

The terms in which workers are 'blamed' for the crisis are false ones, borrowed uncritically from ruling-class ideology. To acknowledge that trade union strength can have adverse effects on a capitalist economy does not play into the hands of the ruling class. Quite the contrary. The fact that workers' defensive actions can have contradictory effects within capitalism is one reason why the labour movement can ultimately further its interests only by overthrowing the system.

The importance of the transition period

It is impossible to disentangle the various factors discussed above, or to gauge the relative importance of their contributions to the decline of UK competitiveness. But the transition from war to boom was quite clearly a vital one for the development of all major capitalist economies. The specific *form* of transition in each economy was crucial to the performance subsequently achieved.

Once a pattern of low growth had been established in the UK in the early fifties, it developed its own dynamic. If the period that followed had been one of economic, social or political instability we might have had a different story. But it was the most rapid, sustained and tranquil period of economic growth in the history of capitalism. In these circumstances, the internal 'narrowly economic' dynamics of the accumulation process dominated developments overall.

The low rate of accumulation established in the late forties and early fifties hobbled growth of the domestic market. Slow growth offered little incentive for innovative investment, reinforced the co-operative marketing behaviour born of controls and deterred capital from undertaking major greenfield capacity extensions. Inertia had become inbuilt and self-reinforcing.

This self-reproducing pattern of slow growth hardened worker resistance. The sluggishness of markets meant that new, labour-saving techniques generally brought redundancies in their wake. In this context the labour movement treated talk about how good a high productivity, high wage economy along American lines would be, as irrelevant day-dreaming at best, and at worst, cynical propaganda intended to mobilise public opinion behind attempts to break shop floor organisation. It got the short shrift it deserved.

6: Profitability in the Sixties

	Company profits as percentage of company output	Rate of profit for industrial and commercial companies	
		before tax %	after tax %
1960	23.0	14.2	8.9
1965	19.8	11.8	6.4
1970	14.8	8.7	4.9

Source: National Income and Expenditure, *various issues;* Bank of England Quarterly Bulletin, *December 1978, p. 51.*

The profits squeeze of the late sixties

The gentle decline in profitability which had characterised the fifties and early sixties accelerated from the mid-sixties onwards (see Table 6 opposite).

Causes and significance of the squeeze

The causes of this accelerated decline differed from those of the earlier, more gentle one. The sharper fall in profits was not the result of accelerated accumulation in a situation of labour shortage. Indeed, the mid-sixties first saw significant unemployment.

The cause lay in further deterioration in competitiveness. Continued slow productivity growth relative to competitors abroad compelled capitalists to hold the rate at which prices rose below that of costs (primarily wages) in an attempt to retain markets. Profits suffered as a consequence.

But paring down profit margins was not enough to prevent a serious loss of markets. The UK's share of world exports fell and import penetration rose. The loss of markets in a context of continued steady accumulation provoked accelerated scrapping. Unemployment followed.

The major developments of the late sixties were:

- The maintenance of the existing rate of accumulation. Accumulation in manufacturing was 3.6 per cent a year for the period 1960–65 and 3.7 per cent for 1965–70.
- The maintenance (or fractional increase in) the rate of productivity growth. Productivity in manufacturing rose by 3.2 per cent a year in the period 1960–64 and by 3.4 per cent in the period 1964–69.
- A widening of the gap between investment levels in the UK and elsewhere (Table 7).
- A widening of the gap between productivity growth in the UK and elsewhere. Manufacturing productivity in the EEC 'big five', for example, accelerated from an annual rate of growth of 4.8 per cent between 1960 and 1964 to one of 5.9 per cent between 1964 and 1969.

7: Investment Per Head in Manufacturing

	Indices (UK = 100)	
	1965	1970
Belgium	168	203
France	197	238
Italy	80	124
Netherlands	169	270
Japan	100	218
USA	364	355

Source: Blackaby, p. 247.

- A widening of the gap in the quality of technologically advanced products between the UK and its major competitors: 'a one ton basket of German mechanical engineering exports was by 1976 worth about 60 per cent more than a representative ton of British exports, not the 12 per cent more they were worth in 1963, while the rate of tonnages exported remained almost unchanged' (Stout, p. 185).
- A declining share of foreign markets. The UK's share of world exports fell from 14.4 per cent in 1964 to 10.8 per cent in 1970.
- A declining share of the domestic market. Import penetration of the UK market rose from 11.9 per cent in 1964 to 14.8 per cent in 1970.
- Rising unemployment. Employment fell by 0.2 per cent a year between 1964 and 1970 whilst the labour force continued to grow slowly.
- An acceleration of the profits squeeze (see Table 6 page 52).

Trade unions, wages and inflation

What contribution did pay bargaining and wage costs make to sliding competitiveness? The answer is not much.

Over the time span considered in this chapter, pay deal patterns were far less significant than productivity trends in determining changes in competitiveness. The UK slipped between the early fifties and late sixties from being a high-wage economy to a low-wage one, but this was insufficient to offset the negative effect of slow productivity growth on competitiveness.

And, contrary to popular belief, trade unions and pay bargaining had little direct effect on average UK wage costs in the fifties and early sixties. As explained above, the labour shortage made a certain growth in real wages necessary to bring about sufficient scrapping of old plant to release workers to operate newly-installed machines.

Pay bargaining could have yielded a different outcome. If trade unions had won better pay deals, one of two things would have happened. If capitalists had been able to pass on their higher wage costs in prices, there would have been inflation, damaging competitiveness. If prices had not risen, unemployment would have gone up as extra scrapping took place. In fact, prices remained fairly stable and full employment was more or less maintained. So wages rose about as fast as would have happened in a competitive labour market, had everything else been equal.

Trade unions were not irrelevant to the pattern of wages during this period, however. Indirectly, they influenced both the level and form of accumulation, and hence the demand for labour and the rate at which real wages grew. They also influenced the proportion of wages taken in tax, a political decision influenced by the strength and militancy of the working class. But overall, the importance of trade unions in the development of wages at this time is generally exaggerated in extent and misunderstood in form.

The situation changed somewhat in the late sixties. Rising unemployment indicates that trade unions were able to hold real wages above the level they would have settled at in a fully competitive labour market. If wages had adjusted to the level balancing job supply and demand, there would have been less scrapping and higher profits.

In this context capital, through the state in particular, tried out a whole battery of devices to hold down real wages. These included incomes policies, a switch in the burden of taxation from capital to labour and devaluation (whose effect is to reduce real wages by raising import prices and thus the price of consumer goods).

One important outcome of this struggle was the onset of inflation. The 1967 devaluation furnishes a classic example of the mechanisms involved. The rise in import prices hit living standards. Workers reacted by demanding increased money wages, and were strong enough to win. Capitalists responded by raising prices and the state expanded the money supply to avoid a credit squeeze and recession. The result was inflation.

The 1967 devaluation was only one cause of inflation. The combination of slow productivity growth, decreasing competitiveness and a strong working class is inherently inflationary, since raising prices is one of capital's most important devices for offsetting money wage increases. This is not to say that 'trade unions cause inflation' in any simple sense, and certainly not to blame them. But to deny that wage bargaining can play any role in the inflationary process, as do many on the left, is both misleading and dangerous.

This heightened struggle over wages was the prelude to the major class confrontations which were to take place under the Heath government.

3.
The Tories 1970–74

By the end of the sixties the capitalist class and its political representatives were acutely aware of the need to stem the accelerating decline of UK capital. But they were unsure how to go about it. At the heart of their dilemma lay an awareness of the contradictory requirements of production and realisation (Chapter 1). The central problem they faced was whether to use demand management tools to restrict output growth and create unemployment, aiming to improve conditions for producing surplus value, or to expand the economy and improve realisation conditions.

The Tories initially opted for restrictive policies, to hold down wages and prompt rationalisation of industry in response to slow market growth. The tendency for unemployment to hold down wages was to be reinforced by legal restrictions on trade unions, and the government intended the bankruptcies that would inevitably accompany rationalisation to be accepted without intervention. The forces of the market were to be strengthened by returning sections of the nationalised industries to the private sector and by entry into the Common Market (EEC), which would reduce protection against foreign capital.

This strategy which amounted to an almost exclusive concentration on improving conditions for producing surplus value, ran into severe difficulties on all fronts. Such rationalisation as took place was insufficient to restore competitiveness and was achieved only at the expense of considerable stagnation in the economy. Unemployment and legal controls failed utterly to weaken or demoralise the trade unions. Industrial non-intervention proved politically impossible.

The Heath government then did a U-turn and embarked on a policy of expansion to improve realisation conditions. Reliance on market forces was also reduced in favour of increased government intervention in the economy. But this second strategy proved equally ineffective. Working class resistance to Tory policies came to a climax with the miners sending Heath packing. It was the first time in UK history that industrial action had brought down a government.

All in all, the 1970–74 Tory government was an unmitigated disaster for the ruling class.

Phase one: Selsdon Man

The first phase of Tory economic policy was thrashed out at Selsdon Park shortly before the 1970 general election. Heath's opponents coupled venue and flavour of policies. They dubbed him 'Selsdon Man'.

Deflation

The economy was hardly booming when the Tories took office. Unemployment was rising by 4,000–5,000 per month. Output and investment were stagnant. Wages had accelerated rapidly over the previous year as workers tried to make up for the Labour government's years of wage restraint. *The Economist* in its pre-Budget advice (27 March 1971) described the situation as follows:

> Collective bargaining, which is now a completely unregulated monopoly force, has pushed wage earnings up by 14 per cent compared with a year ago while production has barely increased. Prices have risen by about $8\frac{1}{2}$ per cent in a year. But this means company profits have dropped sharply. Both domestic and foreign businessmen are therefore cutting back their investment in Britain at an accelerating rate.

Capital was unsure how to respond. *The Economist* called for money-supply increases to be restricted to 6 per cent a year and the CBI warned against significant expansion, which it argued could not be achieved 'without adding appreciably to inflationary pressures'. But it opposed further deflation on the grounds that it would not hold down wages.

Chancellor Barber disagreed. He accepted the CBI's demands for cuts in surtax and tax on investment income and for granting allowances for interest payments and so on. But he offset their expansionary effect by raising charges for school meals, prescriptions, food and rent by around £500 million. Free school milk was also axed (Margaret Thatcher's first claim to fame).

In an article headlined 'High unemployment now seen as government's main short-term economic plan' Peter Jay (*The Times*, 26 April 1971) wrote that Barber had 'made it quite clear by implication that unemployment as a weapon against inflation [for which read 'wage increases'] has now clearly taken priority over restoration of business confidence and investment'. Barber himself said of the Budget:

> My broad aim is that these measures should after a time slow down and later stop the rise in unemployment; but of course the progress of that aim depends on the progress of de-escalation (of wage increases) . . . later, when pay settlements have returned to more sensible levels it should be safe to allow output to grow at a rate sufficient to reduce the level of unemployment.

For the moment any expansion to reduce unemployment would, he said, be 'irresponsible'.

The measures had the desired effect on employment and growth. Unemployment continued to rise and in the winter of 1971–72 reached a million for the first time since the war. Manufacturing investment fell by 10 per cent between the first quarter of 1971 and that of 1972.

Profits remained fairly flat. However they did not decline as the deflation began to bite, and spare capacity rose, suggesting an underlying improvement to be reaped in any subsequent expansion, providing only that wage increases could be held in check. But this did not happen. After some deceleration in 1971, wages began to surge forward again in 1972 in the wake of the miners' strike.

Wages policy

The Tories came to power thoroughly hostile to direct government regulation of wages and immediately abolished Labour's Pay and Prices Commission. They intended to rely instead on unemployment and legal controls over trade unions to curtail wage increases. But they soon ran into problems.

Immediately after taking office the new government was faced with a national docks strike which it chose to tackle by staging a Court of Inquiry and declaring a state of emergency – a device seldom used previously in the UK, and then only in extreme situations. Troops were shipped back from Northern Ireland. This response set the pattern for the next few months.

While waiting for unemployment to bite and the Industrial Relations Bill to become law – a process which took 20 months – the government took a tough stand keen to 'set an example', as the employment minister Robert Carr put it, by paying each group of public sector workers a pay increase 1 per cent below the previous one. This policy became known as 'the n-1 norm'.

The strategy was put to the test in September 1970 when 125,000 local authority workers struck. A Committee of Inquiry awarded them most of their claim, arguing that a smaller increase would lead to 'a deterioration in their position without a significant benefit to the country as a whole'. There followed a series of humiliating defeats for the government.

More than a million days were 'lost' in an unofficial miners' strike which won a £3 per week increase. Shortly afterwards, electricity supply workers were granted an increase of around 15 per cent by the Wilberforce Committee. In the private sector, the Ford workers won an £8 per week increase, spread over two years, after a strike in April 1971 involving the 'loss' of two million working days.

The only victories for government policy were the hard-won Post Office and municipal workers' settlements. The Post Office strike which was settled at 9 per cent, about half the claim and only 1 per cent above the government target figure, involved the 'loss' of $6\frac{1}{4}$m working days, the most in any single dispute since 1926.

The n-1 policy was finally buried by the National Union of Mineworkers' strike of 9 January 1972. The dispute led to another declaration of state of emergency, a rota of power cuts in which $1\frac{1}{2}$m workers were laid off, and yet another Court of Inquiry presided over by Wilberforce. The inquiry recommended an increase of about 18 per cent. The miners' executive initially rejected the offer, but additional minor concessions on attendance terms and holidays, wrested from the Prime Minister at the last minute, brought acceptance.

The claim was won largely by highly effective picketing. By early February pickets were blockading power stations and preventing the entry not only of coal, but also of other essential supplies, such as hydrogen and oil. The decisive struggle took place at the Saltley Coke Depot in Birmingham. A hundred thousand tons of coke were stored at the depot, which, by the end of January was loading more than half as many lorries again as normal.

Local pickets were reinforced by Yorkshire miners and on Monday, 7 February, the picket reached 2,000 strong. 47 lorries were loaded. On the Tuesday, 12 pickets and 6 policemen were injured as the police had to fight every lorry through individually. Of 50 which tried to get through, only 39 succeeded. On the Wednesday, 43 lorries were loaded. On the Thursday, in response to a call for support from Yorkshire miners' leader, Arthur Scargill, local engineering and other workers swelled the picket to 15,000 and at 10.45 the depot was locked on police instructions. Over the six days, 76 people had been arrested, 61 of them miners.

The miners' victory had a traumatic effect on the government. Brendan Sewill, an advisor to Barber, describes its feeling as follows:

> At the time many of those in influence looked into the abyss and saw only a few days away the possibility of the country being plunged into a state of chaos not so very far removed from that which might prevail after a minor nuclear attack. If that sounds melodramatic I need only say that with the breakdown of power supplies, food supplies, sewage, communications, effective government and law and order, it was the analogy which was used at the time. That is the power that exists to hold the country to ransom: it was fear of that abyss which had an important effect on subsequent policy. (Sewill, p. 50).

The Industrial Relations Act

The n-1 norm had been intended only as a stop-gap show of strength while unemployment grew, and began to exercise a restraining influence on wage militancy. The government's real hope for controlling the unions lay in its proposed industrial relations legislation. When this did become law, it proved an even greater fiasco than the failure of the n-1 norm.

The Industrial Relations Act aimed to restrict union power, and to re-establish full-time trade union officials' control over shop stewards. There were what Robert Carr called 'eight central pillars' which the government considered to be non-negotiable. The government was to:

1. Outlaw the closed shop, with minor exceptions.
2. Require trade unions to register with a newly created Registrar of Trade Unions and Employees Associations as a condition for maintaining important legal rights. Registration would involve full specification of the circumstances under which strikes could be called and of the powers and duties of shop stewards. This provision was intended to force the unions to limit the authority of stewards, for fear that their actions could lead to claims against the unions for 'unfair industrial practices', and to intimidate stewards, who would be liable as individuals for unfair industrial practices if they exceeded their authority.
3. Treat all collective agreements not including a written statement to the contrary as legally binding contracts.
4. Remove legal immunity for sympathetic strikes, a provision with 'widespread implications for blacking and picketing'.
5. Grant the Secretary of State the right to order the postponement of industrial action for up to 60 days (a 'cooling-off' period) and to insist on a ballot of the membership prior to action if a dispute threatened 'the life of the nation'.
6. Establish a special procedure under which binding arrangements for conducting disputes could be imposed.
7. Grant trade unions the right to recognition only after investigation by the Commission on Industrial Relations.
8. Establish a procedure for determining which unions should represent workers in particular 'bargaining units'.

The act has been described by Elliot as 'an attempt to solve the "strike problem" by severely restricting the right to strike' and as 'the strongest attack since the last century on rights of collective organisation and collective action' (Elliot p. 581).

There was strong opposition to the act from trade unionists. The TUC organised a national publicity campaign against the Bill and a demonstration on 21 February 1971 in London which drew about 140,000 workers. Although the TUC rejected strike action, there were protest strikes of 350,000 on 8 December 1970, 170,000 on 12 January 1971, and $1\frac{1}{4}$m on 1 March and again on 18 March.

The TUC Special Conference in Croydon on 18 March 1971,

'strongly advised' a complete boycott of the act – refusal to register, to enter into legally enforceable agreements or to co-operate with the National Industrial Relations Court (NIRC) or the Commission on Industrial Relations. The TUC Conference in September passed a motion from the Amalgamated Union of Engineering Workers and the Transport and General Workers' Union instructing unions to de-register. All the big unions did so, although the shopworkers and local government workers dragged their feet.

Shortly after the act became law, the three railway unions put in a claim for 16 per cent. Their response to an 11 per cent offer was a work-to-rule and overtime ban. The government applied to the NIRC and obtained a 14-day cooling-off period. Sir John Donaldson, President of the NIRC and a Tory lawyer, ordered a return to normal working. The unions agreed but promised more industrial action immediately the 14 days lapsed.

On 11 May 1972, the government applied to the NIRC for a compulsory ballot. The TUC granted the unions the right to defend themselves in the NIRC but lost both the initial case and an appeal to the High Court. So the ballot went ahead – and yielded a six-to-one majority in favour of further industrial action. The unions settled for 13 per cent, the evening before they planned to resume their work-to-rule and overtime ban. So the act's first outing gave the government a humiliating defeat.

The next battle involved dock workers imposing unofficial blacking on certain container terminals. It began with Donaldson's judgement that the Transport and General Workers' Union would be responsible for their stewards' unofficial action at Heaton's Liverpool terminal unless it withdrew their credentials or expelled them. The judgement was set aside by the Appeal Court on 2 June. The Appeal judgement implied that since the unions were not liable for the stewards' actions, legal proceedings could be taken against the individuals concerned.

On 12 June an order was obtained to halt picketing at the Chobham Farm container depot. Three workers went on picketing and would have been imprisoned had it not been for the mysterious Official Solicitor. This hitherto-unheard-of figure appeared uninvited on their behalf and had the order quashed by the Court of Appeal on grounds of insufficient evidence. This intervention 'averted country-wide extension of strikes, which were already beginning' (Wigham, p. 162).

The Midland Cold Storage Company, owned by the Vestey family, brought the next case. Midland had closed down warehouses for property development, putting 49 dockers out of work, and had opened up a container depot in which it had reached a closed-shop agreement with the shopworkers union, which it described as being 'more realistic'. Midland was saving about £400 per week by not using dock labour.

On the basis of evidence obtained by private detectives, Donaldson put five dockers in Pentonville Prison on 21 July. 44,000 dockers and 130,000 other workers protested with strike action. The TUC General Council, under tremendous pressure from activists, called a one-day general strike for 31 July.

The Official Solicitor made another appearance and asked Donaldson to review the case. Fortunately for the Official Solicitor, on the same day, and much earlier than expected, the House of Lords upheld Donaldson's original decision that the primary means of enforcement contemplated in the act concerned the funds of organisations, rather than individuals, and that shop stewards had implied authority from their union to take action. This decision let the government off the hook, since Donaldson could then argue that the law now held unions, rather than individual pickets, responsible. He released the Pentonville five and the one-day strike was called off. This episode justified *The Times*'s description of the act as a 'disordered slot-machine which produced a succession of unforeseen results, mostly raspberry flavoured'.

The final skirmish over the act was with the Amalgamated Union of Engineering Workers, which was fined first £5,000 and then £50,000 on 1 December 1972, for refusing membership to one James Goad. The NIRC ordered the seizure of £100,000 from AUEW funds and fined the union £75,000 for contempt of court over its refusal to stop a recognition strike at Conmech. The labour correspondent of the *Economist* pointed out that in the AUEW 'those who opposed the union's rigid policy were discredited and moderates everywhere found they had been undermined' (Milligan, p. 73).

By this time, the actions of the NIRC had become an

embarrassment to the government. The court granted only one injunction in the nine months after September 1972 as compared with eight in the previous nine months. One study reported that 'it was widely believed by the managers and trade unionists whom we interviewed that from the end of 1972 onwards, the government wanted to avoid as far as possible the use of the controversial sections of the act against unions or individuals' (Weekes et al. p. 228). The government made no further attempts to use the cooling-off period or ballot provisions.

One important effect of the act was to encourage political strikes, which had begun under the previous Labour government with a demonstration on May Day 1969 against Barbara Castle's employment law reform proposals, *In Place of Strife*, and a strike of 22,000 dockers against Labour's proposals for nationalising the ports in March 1970. Between July 1970 and July 1974, more than 3m days were 'lost' in protest strikes against the Industrial Relations Bill, more than 1m against NIRC decisions and 1.6m against incomes policy.

Hiving off and the nationalised industries

The Tories' attempt to 'discipline' the unions and hold down the rate of wage increases had failed utterly. The overall strategy could therefore succeed only if market forces prompted a process of thorough rationalisation in response to stagnation. One policy partly intended to effect such a process was that of 'hiving off' – returning profitable sections of the nationalised industries to the private sector.

The 1970 Tory election manifesto outlined the policy as follows:

> We will progressively reduce the involvement of the State in the nationalised industries, for example, the steel industry, so as to improve their competitiveness. An increasing use of private capital will help to reduce the burden on the tax payer, get better investment decisions, and ensure more effective use of total resources.

In the summer of 1970 John Davies, Minister for Industry, spelled out plans for the British Steel Corporation (BSC) in more detail. The government was, he said, considering selling the chemical, constructional engineering and so-called 'peripheral' activities of BSC to private capital. The remainder (bulk iron and steel making) was to be divided into two corporations, which would compete both with each other and with private producers at home and abroad. BSC management was appalled by the proposals.

By April 1971 the idea of splitting BSC had been dropped following an inquiry by the Department of Trade and Industry, which presumably revealed its lunacy. In June 1971, BSC was given the go-ahead for a full short-term investment programme and allowed to *acquire* substantial assets in Firth Brown, to rationalise the special steels industry. It retained its chemical and constructional engineering sections, which might (but in the event did not) solicit some private capital. All BSC lost were its wire interests, which were exchanged for shares in British Ropes.

Finally, in December 1972, after months of haggling a £3,000m expansion programme was announced to extend capacity to 36m tonnes by the early eighties – an increase of 40 per cent. Some 23,000 jobs were to be lost as old capacity was phased out, to add to the 30,000 which went with (re)nationalisation in 1967. The *Financial Times* reported (19 December 1972) that 'even these figures would look relatively insignificant, however, if the Corporation is allowed to phase out obsolete capacity and bring in new steel-making plant at the rate it has proposed'.

The steel industry's strategic nature compelled the Tories to abandon their plans to hive off sections of it. Instead, they undertook a major modernisation programme. The hiving-off policy was limited to Thomas Cook and another travel firm, some NCB brickworks and the government-owned Carlisle pubs.

Tory policy on nationalised industries then took other tacks. The government intervened in March 1971 to halve a proposed 14 per cent steel price rise and subsequently pressured the nationalised industries to adopt the CBI's policy of restricting price rises to 5 per cent. This move was presented as an attempt to contain inflation. It would be more accurate to describe it as an attempt to hold down the cost of steel to private capital.

It would be incorrect, however, to view Tory policy as essentially one of holding down nationalised industry prices to provide cheap inputs for capital, hence increasing private sector profits. The effects of low nationalised industry prices on profits are more complex than they appear.

Charging capital low prices for nationalised industry output does not alter the volume of surplus value produced in the economy as a whole (including the nationalised industries). It allows industries purchasing cheap inputs to appropriate higher profits than would otherwise be the case. But it does so only by reducing profits elsewhere correspondingly.

The profits which suffer in the first instance are those of the nationalised industries themselves. The rate of profit for these industries as a whole was indeed very low under the Tories, averaging less than 1 per cent between 1970 and 1974. Even this low rate was achieved only by putting up government subsidies to nationalised industries, from £175m in 1970 to £654m in 1973. Without these subsidies, the rate of profit would have fallen from 0.3 per cent in 1970 to minus 2 per cent in 1973.

Thus far, capital appears to gain from low nationalised industry prices. With the state sector taking a disproportionately small amount of the surplus, more is available to capital. The rate of profit in the private sector becomes significantly higher than would otherwise be the case.

But the nationalised industries have to finance their invest-ment programmes (and the government has to find money to pay subsidies to them). If capital is taxed to finance the nationalised industries, it loses in tax what it gains from low nationalised industries' prices. If the government borrows from capital to finance the nationalised industries' deficit, capital cannot use its higher profits for productive investment. Only if capital can force the working class to bear the cost of financing the nationalised industries through higher taxation does it clearly gain.

Though the effect of holding down nationalised industries' prices is problematic, that of increasing their efficiency is not. For if productivity can be increased, and hence the cost of inputs to the private sector held down without increased borrowing, then total surplus value is increased. Private capital receives higher profits without any need to channel them back to the nationalised industries.

Government pressure on nationalised industries to use 'commercial pricing criteria' and achieve a rate of profit comparable to that of the private sector is only superficially concerned with pricing. The main aim is to pressurise the industries into increasing efficiency and raising productivity. The Tories retreated over hiving off sections of BSC because they realised that direct government pressure would yield rationalisation more effectively than would the ideologically preferable approach of partial de-nationalisation.

Lame ducks

The policy of relying on the operation of market forces to bring about extensive rationalisation in the context of stagnant markets required the government to accept that weak sections of capital would go bankrupt. The Tories were aware of this and initially decided not to prop up ailing firms. John Davies, Minister for Industry, said at the 1970 Party Conference that he would 'not bolster or bail out companies where I can see no end to the process of propping them up'.

In a memorandum of January 1970, Nicholas Ridley, appointed by Heath to formulate shipbuilding policy and later to become Davies's hatchet-person, argued that no more money should be given to Upper Clyde Shipbuilders (UCS). After the resulting bankruptcy:

> We could put in a Government 'Butcher' to cut up UCS and sell cheaply to Lower Clyde and others the assets of UCS to minimise upheaval and dislocation . . . After liquidation or reconstruction as above, we should sell the Government holding in UCS even for a pittance. (quoted Buchan, p. 44).

In the event, the government's about-turn on this 'lame duck' policy was arguably the most blatant and dramatic of its policy reversals. As Ridley subsequently admitted (*Sunday Times*, 20 January 1974), the struggle at UCS forced the government to change its mind.

In February 1971 the government, in the midst of the Rolls Royce crisis, agreed to extend credit to UCS. This allowed the most profitable section of the yards to be sold to Yarrow for the nominal sum of £1, in return for which Yarrow received a £4½m loan. The government refused UCS's request for £5–6m working capital in June, and set up a Committee of Inquiry which said that since the yards had been amalgamated in 1968, 'no improvement in facilities, no worthwhile investment has been made. Facilities remain as they were before the merger, ill-equipped and cramped at Clyde, less out-of-date but still more cramped at Scotstoun and even at Govan by no means modern' (quoted Buchan, p. 155).

The government accepted the Committee's recommendation to close two of the four UCS yards with the loss of 6,000 out of 8,500 jobs. John Davies said in the Commons that even this would require 'more productive and realistic' working arrangements and wage levels.

A 'work-in' at the yards, supported by two one-day strikes of about 160,000 workers in Scotland put pressure on the government. Eventually, three of the yards were incorporated into Govan shipbuilders, with a government grant of £35m (nearly £8m had already been given to the liquidator) and the fourth yard was sold to Marathon, an American firm, with extra government support worth £12m.

The episode was humiliating for Davies. When Govan became operative in July 1972 he was forced to guarantee support for 'five years or until the company is on its feet'. At the same time it wasn't a simple victory for the UCS workers as over 2,000 jobs were lost.

The nationalisation of Rolls Royce in February 1971, after what the *Guardian* described as the 'most spectacular crash in living memory', was an even more traumatic reversal of the lame duck policy, in that it involved one of British capital's few 'blue-chip' firms. But the retreat was accomplished quickly and Davies could argue that the unique nature of the aircraft industry (particularly huge R & D expenses) justified this particular exception to the general policy of disengagement.

The fundamental problem at Rolls Royce was fierce competition from the US giants, against which the price of the crucial RB 211 engine had been pared down to a level quite unprofitable once launch costs rose from an estimated £65m in 1968 to more than £250m by 1971. The Rolls Royce failure was thus an extreme example of British capital's inability to stand up to foreign competition.

The solution – nationalisation 'at a stroke' – enabled

socialists to point out how rapidly the 'parliamentary process' had been sidestepped by capital and could in future be short-circuited by the labour movement. But, although the jobs of between 12,000 and 18,000 workers employed on the RB 211 project were saved, for 4,300 others nationalisation meant the dole queue.

The extent of rationalisation achieved

Despite all the setbacks and reversals, capital did achieve considerable rationalisation during this period. There was a spate of closures of old plant mostly during the recession year of 1971. This alone would have raised average productivity, by eliminating machinery on which output per worker was particularly low. But more important was an extensive 'shake-out' of labour.

Redundancies involving 1,000 or more workers noted by *The Times* during 1971 included all the spectacular bankruptcies – Rolls Royce, Vehicle and General Insurance, the *Daily Sketch*, UCS and Lines Brothers (toys). Literally dozens of major firms declared redundancies of 500 or more.

Manufacturing employment fell sharply between 1970 and 1972, while output rose a little. But the full benefit of the 'shake-out' was felt only in the upswing of 1973, when substantial increases in output were achieved with virtually no increase in employment. Between 1970 and 1972, employment in manufacturing fell by 6.8 per cent while output rose by 2.0 per cent. Between 1972 and 1973, manufacturing employment rose by 0.7 per cent, while output shot up by 8.3 per cent.

Rationalisation was equally successful in the nationalised industries. Despite falls in investment which generally exceeded those in private manufacturing, productivity in the nationalised industries rose nearly as fast as in manufacturing as a whole (and far faster in British Gas and Post Office Telecoms). The increases were once again achieved primarily by cuts in employment, averaging 9 per cent for the nationalised industries as a whole.

The U-turn

Productivity per person per hour in manufacturing rose by 5 per cent in 1971, a rate quite comparable to British capital's competitors. Substantial rationalisation was thus achieved during the early years of the Tory government, proving that the strategy was working to some extent at least on one crucial front. Yet it was abandoned in 1972.

The most important reason for the reversal was the strong, effective working-class resistance described above.

Further, such rationalisation as had been achieved could provide the basis for a sustained improvement in competitiveness only if an investment boom took place. Deflationary policies, which held back any increase in profits (see Table 1 below) and offered capital no prospect of expanding markets, did not provide the right climate for increasing the rate of accumulation.

1: Rate of Profit: UK, 1970–73

	%
1970	8.7
1971	8.7
1972	8.6
1973	7.2

2: Rates of Growth of Output and Manufacturing Investment: UK, 1970–72

	Rate of growth of output %	Rate of growth of manufacturing investment %
1971	2.4	—6.5
1972	1.4	—13.4
1973	8.1	3.1

Source: Economic Trends *1979 Supplement; Bank of England,* Quarterly Bulletin, *December 1978.*

Capital, well aware of this, was led to oppose large elements of the Tories' strategy and to push for major policy changes. After the debacle over the Industrial Relations Act, for example,

Campbell Adamson of the CBI, who had originally hailed the act as 'the greatest landmark in our industrial history' denounced it as having 'sullied every relationship at national level between unions and employers' and argued for its repeal before the 1974 General Election.

By 1972, capital had also come out in favour of reversing demand-management policies in an attempt to improve the conditions for realisation, hoping to stimulate investment. The CBI said at the time of the 1972 budget:

> Our recent levels of industrial investment and the age of our equipment compare poorly with those of our main European competitors . . . The real returns of a large range of firms are inadequate to pay for the upkeep of assets employed . . . If this state of affairs is allowed to continue industrial decline and large-scale unemployment are inevitable.

The Economist (13 March 1972) came out even more clearly in favour of expansion:

> So long as unemployment remains near to its socially sickening winter million, the danger of more inflation by giving more jobs should rate lower than the threat of continued stagnation in investment – which carries the danger that through the 1970s as through the 1960s Britain might lose out on yet another decade of technological advance. It follows that Mr Barber should determine next week to take more risks on the side of overshooting 5 per cent [growth] than of undershooting it.

Tory strategy therefore not only failed to reverse the decline of UK capital but also came increasingly to encounter severe opposition from both major classes.

Heath, like any sailor, sensed the way the wind was blowing and decided to change course.

Phase two: going for bust

The core of the policy reversal consisted of a switch from deflationary policies, aimed at improving fairly rapidly the conditions for producing surplus value, to expansionary ones, intended to improve realisation conditions almost immediately. The idea was that expansion would stimulate investment and bring about a long-run improvement in potential surplus value and competitiveness.

Higher employment and better markets would, of course, cause the conditions for producing surplus value to deteriorate in the short-run. The increase in employment would remove any lingering hope that the threat of the dole queue would be sufficient to hold down wages. Market growth, together with the obvious collapse of the 'lame duck' policy, would weaken the effectiveness of intensified competition in enforcing rationalisation. The danger was therefore that deterioration in production conditions would depress investment more than the improved opportunities for realisation stimulated it.

The Tories intended to deal with the danger by instituting further policy changes. They abandoned their objections to income policies and tried to embroil the TUC in negotiations over wage control. To smooth the way for the talks, the Industrial Relations Act was put on ice.

Wage control would, they hoped, ensure that profits received the lion's share of higher incomes provided by expansion. The government was to step up aid to industry to encourage investment, and stressed the virtue of EEC entry as a means of providing both the competitive pressure believed necessary to ensure continued rationalisation and the prospect of expanding markets for internationally competitive firms.

All this added up to a coherent strategy, on paper at least. Unfortunately for the Tories, it proved a disaster in practice.

Expansion

In his April 1972 Budget, Barber cut taxes by £1800m and announced that the money supply, which had been growing at an annual rate of 20 per cent, would continue to expand 'at a rate that is also high by the standards of past years, in order to ensure that adequate finance is available for the extra output'. He also made clear that an 'unrealistic exchange rate' would not be allowed to frustrate his determination to 'sustain sound economic growth and to reduce unemployment'. Finally, public expenditure plans for 1974, which had in 1970 been cut by £960m, were raised in 1971 and 1972 by first £500m, then £1200m.

In terms of securing rapid growth, the expansion was outstandingly successful: output rose by 9.1 per cent between the second half of 1971 and the first half of 1973. But its value to capital was more problematic, as an examination of the pattern of expansion shows (Table 3 below).

3: The Pattern of Expansion: UK, 1971–73

	increase 1971–73 (1975 prices)	
	£ billion	percentage
Total Domestic Production	10026	10.4
private consumption	6157	10.4
private house building	91	3.7
government consumption	1604	8.2
government investment		
nationalised industries	−295	−8.5
other	507	8.6
fixed investment by capital		
manufacturing (excl. metal manufacturing)	−264	−7.3
other	1333	23.7
stockbuilding	2748	
exports	3140	13.6
imports	5736	22.7

Source; National Income and Expenditure *1967–77, tables 2.1, 10.2, 10.7;* Monthly Digest of Statistics, *June 1974, table 8.*

The lopsided boom

The 'Barber Boom' of 1972–73 warrants fairly detailed examination. This is because it shows clearly the difficulties involved in attempting to solve capital's problems by full-blown expansion when the rate of profit is low and the working class determined to defend living standards. Its failure helped convince much of the ruling class that all-out deflation, however unpalatable, was a necessary pre-condition for any future expansion. The programme of the Thatcher government owes much to this experience.

The rapid expansion of exports – by UK standards at least – was largely a product of the world upswing (see Chapter 1). The growth in world trade over these years exceeded that of UK exports.

Imports also rose more rapidly than exports. So competitiveness continued to deteriorate during the upswing. Investment by capital did rise relatively fast. But the rise had an extremely limited effect on future competitiveness.

Firstly, a healthy capitalist boom, capable of becoming self-sustaining, normally involves a fall in the share of output going to the working class. Without such a fall, the incentive for continued accumulation is weak (because the share of profits does not rise) and the resources available for investment become limited once full employment (and/or full capacity utilisation) is reached.

This did not happen in the 1972–73 boom. Private consumption rose as rapidly as total production, so that surplus value did not increase significantly and the share of private-sector output available for accumulation remained more or less constant.

Higher imports, rather than extra domestic production, provided for much of the additional accumulation. In effect, UK capital was financing investment by borrowing from its foreign counterparts, either directly (by contracting Eurodollar loans) or indirectly (via borrowing abroad by banks and the government). The boom therefore increased foreign indebtedness and weakened the balance of payments – thus constraining future expansion.

Secondly, the increase in investment was concentrated in activities and sectors with little impact on competitiveness. Much of it consisted of stockbuilding. The ratio of stocks held to total output rose by a staggering 14 per cent between the last quarter of 1971 and that of 1973. Some increase in stocks is necessary to sustain a higher level of output, but stockbuilding does not in itself help improve productivity or potential surplus value. The motive for excessive stockbuilding of 1972–73 was largely speculation, rather than productive accumulation.

Thirdly, public-sector investment was concentrated in public works and social services rather than in the nationalised industries. Investment in such areas contributes little to raising labour productivity (see page 123).

Finally, private-sector fixed investment was extremely unevenly distributed between industries. Many of the areas registering the largest increases were ones in which investment has almost zero impact on international competitiveness. New office blocks for financial institutions are a prime example.

Fixed investment in the crucial manufacturing sector fell by 9 per cent in real terms, while investment by the finance sector rose by 42 per cent. The fixed capital stock in manufacturing rose by only $5\frac{1}{2}$ per cent over the two years of the boom, while that in distribution and other services grew by 14 per cent.

The primary reason accumulation was concentrated outside manufacturing was that profitability had fallen more sharply in that sector than in others. Between 1964 and 1970, the rate of profit in manufacturing had fallen from 12.0 to 6.8 per cent, while in retailing the drop was from 18.1 to 14.8 per cent, and in wholesaling from 12.6 to 11.1 per cent. This disproportionate fall in manufacturing profits was in turn a product of the continued and rapid deterioration of UK manufacturing competitiveness.

The boom's concentration outside manufacturing also comes across clearly in figures for profit increases. Manufacturing profits rose by only 6 per cent between 1970 and 1973, while in services and construction, the rise was between 30 and 55 per cent. In insurance, banking and finance, the increase was 122 per cent.

The credit explosion

The low rate of accumulation in manufacturing cannot be explained by credit shortages. The years 1971–73 saw the biggest expansion of credit in the history of UK capitalism.

This credit explosion was inaugurated in May 1971 by the introduction of a new framework for monetary policy called 'Competition and Credit Control'. The idea was that the banks would be freed from direct restrictions on the volume of loans made – a device on which governments had increasingly relied during the sixties – in return for which they would abandon the practice of non-competition over interest rates. The Bank of England was to control the volume of credit in the economy by increased intervention in the government bond ('gilt-edged') market. If the Bank wished to restrict credit growth, it would increase sales of government bonds, thereby reducing the volume of cash in the economy and driving up interest rates to choke off lending to the private sector. That was the theory.

In practice the Bank, presumably with the connivance of the government, abandoned any serious attempt at firm credit control. By the second quarter of 1972, the money supply was growing at an annual rate of 31 per cent.

The end of June 1972 witnessed a run on sterling during which £1bn of speculative money was withdrawn from the UK and placed in other currencies in the expectation that the sterling exchange rate would fall. This outflow precipitated a major banking crisis as UK banks suddenly had to find the cash to pay overseas depositors who were withdrawing funds. The Bank of England was compelled to buy £356m worth of government bonds from the banks to ensure their solvency. Even after this episode, the Bank made only feeble attempts to check the credit explosion.

Get rich quick

And so there was ample credit in the context of low profitability in production, and high, uneven rates of inflation. Rich individuals and institutions engaged in speculative activities on a massive scale. Many made enormous sums of money while the going was good. Others lost out when the bubble burst. But the frenzied accumulation of financial assets and property titles did nothing to improve UK competitiveness.

Barber's decision to allow interest payments to be offset against income tax hugely reduced the cost of borrowing for rich individuals and encouraged them to exploit all kinds of tax loopholes. They were not slow to respond to the opportunity. Between July 1971 and July 1973 bank lending to individuals rose by a staggering 175 per cent.

One loophole which attracted a great deal of attention – and money – worked as follows. Someone paying the top income tax rate of 98 per cent could borrow £100,000 for one year at, say, 12 per cent interest for a real cost of only £240 (because the interest payments could be offset against tax). With the £100,000 they could buy a 10 per cent Certificate of Deposit on 1 January which could be sold on 31 December for £109,990 without generating any tax liability because of a loophole whereby the capital gain was not taxable if the Certificate was sold within a year of purchase.

The most dramatic example of the diversion of credit into non-productive avenues was the famous property boom of the early 1970s. Borrowing by property companies rose by about £500m. Prices of City commercial property rocketed under Barber, more than doubling between 1971 and 1973.

Since capital gains of 50 per cent or so a year were made on property it is hardly surprising that even a 5 per cent rise in interest rates in the summer of 1973, following a run on sterling, failed to deter borrowers. The money supply continued to rise at an annual rate of about 30 per cent in the second half of 1973.

Putting on the brakes

It was not until December 1973 that the Bank of England began to exercise effective control over credit expansion. It did so by returning to quantitative controls over bank lending, thereby implicitly admitting that the Competition and Credit Control system was unworkable.

These measures were accompanied by public expenditure cuts of £1200m. As Barber pointed out at the time, these cuts were 'by far the biggest reduction in public expenditure for the succeeding year ever made'. Capital programmes were slashed by one-fifth and current expenditure, including staff costs, by one-tenth.

The cuts were presented as being necessary to reduce oil consumption; OPEC was threatening to reduce supplies. Ironically, given the Tories' subsequent position on the issue (see below, Chapter 5), they put no general arguments for a reduction in public expenditure. As Barber said: 'It is the consumption of fuel and power by the public sector that has to be reduced, but not its employment of people.'

The secondary banking crisis

The sector which felt the credit squeeze most acutely was that of the 'secondary' or 'fringe' banks, subject to controls and codes of practice less strict than those under which the major clearing banks operate. These banks had played a major role in financing the property boom. The onset of the squeeze coincided with the first signs of a downturn in the property market.

Many fringe banks became dangerously over-stretched. Deposits were harder to find and commanded higher interest payments. At the same time property companies found it harder to meet repayment schedules.

The first to experience serious problems was London and Counties Securities. Once its difficulties became known, a run began on other fringe banks. There was a real danger of financial crisis snowballing through the banking system as depositors withdrew funds from all but the most reputable banks.

The Bank of England stepped in and organised a support scheme known as 'the lifeboat'. By the end of 1974, lifeboat loans, provided largely by the clearing banks, totalled £1285m. as the property boom collapsed and banks failed abroad. Those providing lifeboat support may have lost up to £200m, with the rest of the money being recovered slowly as properties were sold. Many millions of pounds were lost by shareholders in banks and property companies which either went into bankruptcy or were taken over in a near-bankrupt state.

Mergers

One by-product of the stock market boom caused by the expansion was a flood of mergers and takeovers. Tycoons competed to use their inflated shares to take over under-valued firms. News of bids dominated the financial press.

Mergers and take-overs in 1972 were worth a record £2532m, exceeding the previous peak of 1968. More than half of them involved take-overs of over £25m. Between 1969 and 1973, the top 50 manufacturing companies increased their share of the top 100's assets from 65 per cent to 67.3 per cent, mainly by mergers.

The government appeared unable to make up its mind about merger policy. At the end of 1970, Davies was said to be considering an enlarged Monopolies Commission under which:

> just about everything could and would be subject to examination: full-blown monopolies, mergers, industrial policies that could not

be said technically to be violating any legislation, service industries, the lot. (*Economist*, 19 December 1970).

But, a year later, the *Economist* reflected on the abandonment of simple free-market theories:

> There is a growing feeling in Whitehall that companies will have to be big if they are to survive in the Common Market. A government should not stop them from growing, but just stop them from misbehaving. (6 November 1971).

The Monopolies Commission did block the Boots-Glaxo merger, forced a squeeze on Cornflakes prices (Kelloggs made a 46 per cent rate of profit in the years 1967–71), and enforced price reductions on the drug company Hoffmann-La Roche (which had been making 70 per cent on capital employed). But such curbs on the 'unacceptable face of capitalism – to use Heath's description of the Lonrho Company – was intended to confirm the acceptability of the rest.

The extent to which the merger boom reflected industrial logic, rather than merely financial speculation, is dubious. In any case, the expansion collapsed before any benefits in terms of rationalisation had a chance to surface.

Capital's attitude to the boom

The shortcomings and contradictions of the boom were in large part obvious at the time. Many commentators remarked on them and criticised Barber's policies sharply. For example, Peter Jay, in *The Times*, 7 May 1973, denounced the 'Boom that must go bust':

> The balance of demand between public and private consumption on the one hand and net exports (exports less imports) and investment on the other is almost certainly more distorted than in any other post-war economic cycle. This means quite simply that when the full employment rate is reached the rate of consumption is so high that far too few resources are left over for the exports to pay for 'full employment' levels of imports and for the rate of investment associated with full employment.

He also pointed to the rise in the money supply, well over 20 per cent a year, geared, he said, 'to limitless accommodation of all credit demands at rates of interest which, after discounting tax relief and income tax, are being kept close to or below nil'.

The CBI had no such criticism. Despite its later protests about the level of government expenditure and state employment, the scale of the public-sector deficit and the need to control the money supply, the CBI was fully in favour of Barber's 'go for bust' policies throughout the boom.

In a reply to Jay (*Times*, 11 May 1973) Campbell Adamson, then Director-General of the CBI, ignored the increase in public expenditure (expected to be 5.3 per cent in real terms that financial year, according to Jay), the government's borrowing requirement (estimated by Jay at 7 per cent of output) and the explosive growth of the money supply. He exuded optimism. The CBI was, he said, 'fully aware that shortage of plant and skilled man-power are becoming more widespread' but was nevertheless confident that 'because of far-reaching structural and behavioural changes, the present boom is controllable . . . industry is now investing strongly and much of this new capacity should be coming on stream towards the middle of next year when it will be most needed'.

In reality, of course, the major 'structural and behavioural change' was the diversion of funds into speculative avenues. Industrial investment was not expanding strongly and new capacity was not needed towards the middle of the following year because, by then, the expansion was over. The argument that the expansion would have continued unchecked had Barber not deflated is unconvincing. Output in the last quarter of 1973 was already $1\frac{1}{4}$ per cent lower than in the first quarter. Although new orders received by contractors for industrial work rose throughout 1973, they were still 8 per cent below the 1970 level in the last quarter. The peak rate of manufacturing investment, reached at the end of 1974, was 7 per cent below that of 1970. Capital was hardly poised for a major burst of accumulation.

The Industry Act

The failure of manufacturing investment to respond to the boom cannot be blamed on Tory meanness when it came to handing out aid to industry. The collapse of the Tories' disengagement policy was cemented by the 1972 Industry Act, which permitted selective financial assistance for individual firms – anathema to right-thinking Tories.

In January 1971, the government had planned to spend £820m on assistance to private industry during 1972–73. This figure was practically doubled, largely as a result of expenditure planned under the act.

In October 1972, Christopher Chataway, Minister of Industry, denounced the view that the government should never assist private industry, saying that those who compete in world markets against 'the American shipbuilding industry which now receives grants of up to 50 per cent on all new orders, against the strongly supported French and German computer industries, against the nationally co-ordinated attack of Japanese industry, against the American micro-electronic industry . . . find it hard to understand how such nostalgic attitudes can still survive. The British government is no longer setting the rules within which British industry competes for imperial markets'. This statement reflected the opinion of the section of British capital which understood it was impossible to compete without massive state aid.

Chataway's position was also shaped by pressure from the Labour movement. He argued that 'to allow a major firm to collapse in an area of high unemployment, where the cost of putting the firm on its feet will definitely be less than the cost of paying unemployment benefit, is clearly bad economic, as well as social, policy', and even went so far as to say that 'it is reasonable to back less certain winners where rates of unemployment are highest' (*The Times*, 13 October 1972).

Two months later, 200 applications had been received for selective assistance under sections 7 and 8 of the act. The act was virtually a blank cheque, allowing for aid to a firm 'when it may benefit the economy, is regarded as being in the national interest or when funds cannot be provided from other sources'. (*The Times*, 13 December 1972).

CBI fears that the Industry Act would be used in an interventionist fashion – that is, to give aid only with strings attached – proved groundless. The act provided a convenient means of further subsidising the private sector, which was already receiving huge hand-outs in the form of 'free depreciation', a device introduced by the Tories which allowed investment to be written off immediately against tax.

The EEC

Because the boom failed to encourage a significant increase in productive investment, the need for effective rationalisation in the use of existing plant became all the more pressing. But the rapid expansion of markets following the U-turn helped relax the pressure of domestic market forces on capital. EEC entry therefore assumed increasing importance in the overall strategy to induce competitive pressures.

Supporters of Common Market entry stressed the supposed benefit of more intense competition from European capital once tariff barriers were lowered. The 1971 White Paper, for example, claimed that the reduction of trade barriers would:

> through increased competition foster the more efficient use of resources over a wide range of industry . . . The abolition of tariffs and the consequent increase in intra [EEC] trade were accompanied by important changes in the performance of manufacturing industries in the six countries. Those industries which competed with imports faced an intensification of competitive pressures as tariffs fell, obliging them to see ways of raising efficiency and reducing costs.

The massive pro-entry campaign was supported by big UK capital, which presumably felt sufficiently strong to compete with other capitals in the Common Market and sufficiently mobile to move production progressively to greener pastures elsewhere in the EEC if the UK's industrial decline continued. The banks, for whom the freedom of movement of money capital was the over-riding consideration, felt the EEC's 'doctrinal dedication to a totally free movement of all factors of production was the sweetest sound the City [had] heard since the end of the war' (Evans, p. 107).

As it turned out, industrial capital proved more able to sample greener grass than to withstand intensified competition. Direct investment abroad rose from £550m in 1970 to £1650m in 1973, while manufacturing imports continued to displace domestic production, rising from 17 per cent of sales in 1970 to 22 per cent in 1973.

Incomes policy

In launching the Barber boom, the Tories abandoned their efforts to hold down wages by creating large-scale unemployment. From the autumn of 1972, the government abandoned reliance on market forces to keep down wage increases and opted for incomes policies instead. It would have preferred the TUC to accept such policies voluntarily, but was compelled to make them statutory.

On 26 September 1972 Heath proposed a package to the TUC consisting of a flat-rate increase in earnings of £2.60 per worker plus an additional 20p 'threshold payment' for every percentage-point increase in the cost of living above six. This package would have yielded average increases in earnings of 8 per cent, and a significant rise in living standards, if the government's 5 per cent inflation target had been met.

But it would also have brought about a substantial redistribution to profits if the 5 per cent target for output growth – to be achieved almost entirely by productivity increases – had also been achieved. The *Financial Times* (27 September 1972) reported that the Tories had calculated the policy would reduce the share of output taken by wages to the average level of the previous ten years if these targets were achieved (though the paper's own calculations suggested the government's figures were exaggerated). Inflation over 5 per cent would bring further redistribution to profits since the proposed threshold payments would compensate for only about two-thirds of each percentage point increase in inflation, and that only after prices had risen by more than 6 per cent.

Late summer 1972 was not a good time to seek TUC acceptance of the package. The mass struggles against the Industrial Relations Act had reached their peak not long before and building workers had just won an increase of 15 per cent after their first-ever national industrial action. The dispute had been a lengthy and bitter one, lasting from 26 June to 17 September. Some 3.8m working days were 'lost' and pickets at Shrewsbury jailed for conspiracy.

The only feature of the situation which might conceivably have worked in the Tories' favour was the fact that real take-home pay had risen very rapidly. For the average manual worker in

1972, it was 7.4 per cent higher than in the previous year as a result of big money wage increases following the miners' settlement, reinforced by tax cuts. This increase exceeded that of the whole period from 1964–70. But even this feature of the situation was double-edged; workers might have viewed it as evidence that militancy paid off.

Predictably, the TUC rejected the package and put forward alternative proposals. These included an extra £1.40 on pay, an increase in the size of threshold payments, to start once inflation exceeded 5 rather than 6 per cent, statutory price controls and a cut of $2\frac{1}{2}$ percentage points in VAT. The TUC also demanded measures to check land speculation, the end of rent increases under the Housing Finance Act, a wealth tax, a surcharge on capital gains and limitations on dividends, higher family allowances and the suspension of the Industrial Relations Act.

Equally predictably, Heath rejected the TUC's package. It would have been politically humiliating for the government to accept. It would also have negated the whole point of the exercise – the TUC's proposals would not have had the required effect on profits.

When negotiations collapsed, Heath imposed a statutory freeze on pay, prices and dividends. During the five months of the freeze, average earnings rose by less than 1 per cent, while prices increased by 2.4 per cent. The government made much of price rises being due largely to seasonal foodstuffs costing more. It might as well have told workers unemployed during the winter that, viewed in 'seasonally-adjusted' terms, they were not on the dole.

The freeze was followed by Phase II of Heath's incomes policy. This set a maximum for pay rises of £1 per week plus 4 per cent, with an upper limit of £250 per year.

The first dispute over Phase II concerned the gas workers, whose previous claim had fallen victim to the freeze. They were persuaded back to work by the withdrawal of threatened redundancies and an improvement in pensions. Shortly afterwards, three civil service unions called their first ever one-day national stoppage, involving 128,000 workers, followed by overtime bans. Some 50,000 hospital ancillary workers also took selective strike action. But the TUC had come round to a position of 'reluctant acquiescence' in the policy by the time of its 'day of national protest and stoppage' on 1 May, intended as a focal point of opposition to Phase II. Nonetheless, as many as 1.6m workers took part in the day of action.

The Pay Board claimed that the average increase resulting from approved Phase II settlements was 7⅔ per cent, a figure very close to the government's target. But an examination of national figures indicates that average hourly earnings (excluding over-time) rose by 13½ per cent between October 1972 and October 1973. The discrepancy is explained by payments resulting from settlements postponed by the freeze, the move to equal pay, payment by results systems and annual increments.

Despite the rapid expansion of output, profitability fell by nearly one quarter between the last three months of 1972 and those of 1973.

One cause of this sharp fall lay in wages rising more rapidly than prices. The price index for output as a whole (that most relevant to profitability) increased by only 8.5 per cent between the last quarters of 1972 and 1973. A massive rise of 33 per cent in import prices over the same period also depressed profits. The cost of imports rose because of the world boom in commodity prices (Chapter 1) and a 9 per cent fall in the value of the pound.

Phase III of the Tories' incomes policy, which came into operation in November 1973, again aimed to restrict the rate at which wages grew. Wage rises were limited to £2.25 per week or 7 per cent, whichever was higher, up to a maximum of £350 a year, with additional threshold payments of 40p a week for each percentage point increase in the cost of living in excess of six. If this had been all, sticking to Phase III would have held real wages more or less constant.

But additional clauses allowed further payments for changes in pay structure facilitating the more efficient use of labour, of 'genuine' efficiency schemes, for progress towards equal pay and as compensation for working unsocial hours. (This last provision was intended to avoid a battle with the miners). Total increases, excluding threshold payments, were expected to average around 10–11 per cent, implying average increases in real wages of around 4 per cent.

Overall, then, Phase III was not nearly tough enough to fulfil the interests of capital. Even if everyone had abided by its provisions, it would not have improved profitability significantly. But the government almost certainly regarded it as the best it would achieve in the circumstances. These included a miners' claim for pay rises ranging from 22–46 per cent.

The miners' strike

The National Coal Board responded to the miners' claim with an offer which would have increased the wage bill by 13 per cent and stretched the Phase III rules to the limit. The miners rejected it and began an overtime ban on 12 November.

The rejection surprised Heath, who believed he had reached an understanding with miners' leader Joe Gormley the previous July at a secret meeting – secret from the National Union of Mineworkers' Executive, that is. Gormley had promised to deliver NUM acceptance of the offer providing it contained a large payment for unsocial hours (*Sunday Times*, 22 February 1976).

The government reacted to the setback publicly by taking emergency powers. Against panic surrounding the 66 per cent oil price rise and threatened 25 per cent cut in supplies (Chapter 1), the government announced that manufacturing industry would be allowed to operate for only three days a week from the end of December. It also took other, less public measures:

> Nobody knew it at the time, but in December 1973 Edward Heath's Conservative administration alerted the alternative government that takes over the running of Britain in an extreme national emergency. The anonymous figures who command the military and the Civil Service to keep essential services going – known as the regional commissioners – were put on standby – This had been done to avert a state of chaos . . . Decisions had to be taken about the location of emergency generators in case the power supply failed completely. (*Sunday Times*, 22 February 1976).

John Davies, a minister at the time, told the *Sunday Times*: 'I said to my wife and children that we should have a nice time because I deeply believed that it was the last Christmas of its kind that we would enjoy.'

The effects of the three-day week began to bite in the New Year.

By the middle of January, more than a million workers were on short time. Many more were protected only by guaranteed week provisions, which the CBI tried in vain to suspend.

On 9 January the TUC made an unprecedented offer:

> The General Council accept that there is a distinctive and exceptional situation in the mining industry. If the Government are prepared to give an assurance that they will make possible a settlement between the miners and the NCB, other unions will not use this as an argument in negotiations in their own industry.

Barber rejected it. Heath was apparently close to despair, but many Tories welcomed the prospect of a head-on confrontation. Sir William Armstrong, the civil servant who had become known as the Deputy Prime Minister, 'compared Britain to the Phoenix rising from the ashes of a smash-up and began to define the conflict in military terms.' (*Sunday Times*, 29 February 1976). The terminology was more than rhetoric.

A few weeks earlier, a rumour about Arab terrorists had provided the pretext for an operation at Heathrow Airport involving thousands of troops, armed police, tanks and armoured cars. The *Evening Standard* had confided that 'to an extent' the Heathrow events were

> a public relations manoeuvre aimed at accustoming the public to the sight of troops on the streets . . . It is known that the Ministry for Defence has contingency plans, often under review, for moving in servicemen to take over areas of industry vital to the running of the country.

But the prospect of such a confrontation was not without its dangers for the ruling class. Mick McGahey, the Scottish miners' leader, said on 27 January: 'I will appeal [to the troops] to assist and aid the miners. Troops are not all anti-working class . . . many of them are miners' sons.' The press treated him as if he were inciting treason, but the *Evening Standard* confessed he had posed 'exceptionally delicate questions' about whether troops would obey orders.

As the miners became more determined, it became clearer that there were disagreements within the ruling class on how best to deal with the situation. The miners' vote on strike action showed 81 per cent in favour of national stoppage. The government's response was to promise more negotiations only if the miners formally accepted the principles of Phase III and resumed normal working. In the meantime, it called an election for 7 February, three days before the date the miners' executive had fixed for national strike action.

Heath appealed to the miners to delay the strike until after the election. They refused. An anonymous group of industrialists offered to provide funds to meet their claim, an offer the miners also refused.

The Tory election campaign theme was 'Who runs the country?' Heath's opening broadcast asked: 'Do you want Parliament and the elected government to continue to fight strenuously against inflation? Or do you want them to abandon the struggle against rising prices under pressure from one particularly powerful group of workers?' Barber attacked the Labour Party as taken over by reds, and Carrington, a leading figure in the Tory Party, intervened at the last moment to remove from an election broadcast footage in which pictures of Labour leaders merged into those of Lenin and Mao.

Douglas Hurd, an adviser of Heath's, claimed that: 'Ted's real worry is about the consequences of a Tory landslide. It would sweep away the moderation which post-war Tories went into politics to defend. It would be a triumph for the extremists.'

If that were indeed his main worry (which we doubt) then he was presumably relieved by the results at the polls. The first general election in UK history directly precipitated by industrial action returned a Labour government.

Heath's fears for the Tory Party were, however, borne out in the longer term. The experience of the 1970–74 period in office did assist the rise of the new Tory right, which had gained control of the party by the time of its victory in the 1979 election (see below Chapter 5).

Balance sheet and legacy

The economic record of the 1970–74 Tory government makes dismal reading for the ruling class. UK capital's position worsened on all major fronts. All important economic indicators deteriorated significantly between 1970 and 1973. The rate of profit fell from 8.7 to 7.2 per cent, the share of UK manufacturing exports in world trade declined from 10.8 to 9.4 per cent and the rate of inflation rose from 6.3 to 9.1 per cent. The rate of accumulation in manufacturing averaged a paltry 2.2 per cent over the period, half the EEC rate and one-sixth of that in Japan.

Workers, on the other hand, generally did well under the Tories. Real take-home pay rose by 3.5 per cent a year between 1970 and 1973, four times the rate achieved under the 1964–70 Labour government. The strength and self-confidence of the labour movement also grew enormously. The organised working class proved capable of winning major real-wage increases and neutralising almost all the Tories' moves against it to boot. It mobilised the biggest strike wave since 1926, which culminated in the 1974 general election and the return of a Labour government with a programme well to the left of any pledged by a major party since 1945. The British working class had seldom, if ever, been in a stronger position.

4.
Labour 1974–79

Labour was swept into office in February 1974 on the crest of the biggest wave of industrial militancy in the UK since 1926. Many trade unionists had rightly seen the events of the winter as a major class confrontation involving stakes potentially far higher than the actual wage demands. A substantial number of activists had viewed the struggle primarily as one to bring down the Tories and return a Labour government.

This group, which was sufficiently powerful to dominate trade union and Labour Party policy as laid down by annual conferences, put pressure on the Labour leadership to adopt a radical programme. It was also a powerful force available to assist in its implementation. Its existence was a vital feature of the context in which the new government took office.

The formation of the 1974 Labour government was a major leftward shift in British social democracy. Its manifesto promised a programme considerably more radical than any presented to the UK electorate by a major party since 1945. If it had been fully and successfully implemented, it would have brought about a major redistribution of income and wealth in favour of workers and their dependants. More fundamentally, it would have made substantial inroads into the capitalist class's control over economic activity.

The programme adopted was not the only indication of a leftward swing. The balance within the Parliamentary Labour Party had also shifted significantly in favour of the left. The Tribune group of MPs had more or less doubled in size in comparison to the 1964–70 period. Left-wingers Michael Foot and Tony Benn were appointed to key economic posts in the cabinet in deference to the strength of the left in the Parliamentary Party, the constituency Labour Parties and the trade unions.

But the promise of policies more radical than any seen for 30 years was disappointed. Between 1974 and 1977 the Labour government presided over a larger recorded fall in real wages than during any comparable period in UK history. It slashed plans for improved social service provision and presided over the highest level of unemployment since the 1930s. These savage attacks on working-class jobs and living standards failed to restore British capitalism to health. UK industry declined further and more sharply under Labour than under the Tories.

The Heath government was an unmitigated disaster for the ruling class. The Wilson/Callaghan governments' end of term report showed the bankruptcy of right-wing social democracy, both as a system for offering workers steady improvements in living conditions and as a means of shackling the working class in the interests of capital.

The rise and fall of the Labour left

The move to the left in opposition

During the Heath government, particularly from 1972 onwards, the Labour Party began to develop an extremely radical strategy for state intervention into industry. The core of the programme was the nationalisation of some leading profitable companies and their subsequent operation by a National Enterprise Board.

State control over the operations of private capital was to be strengthened with a system of compulsory planning agreements. All major firms would have to present to the government corporate plans detailing proposed levels of investment, output, employment and so on for approval or amendments. Firms entering these agreements would be required to meet certain broad government objectives (for instance, job creation in the North East) but would themselves decide how to do so. Such a system would represent a halfway house between a centrally planned economy and the unfettered operation of market forces.

The idea of Labour creating a major state holding company, along the lines of the Italian one, was first mooted in 1969. The plan took off in 1972, when it was proposed to Labour's executive committee by two working groups of its industry sub-committee. The chief architect of the proposals was the economist Stuart Holland, and their most powerful champion Tony Benn.

An Opposition Green Paper, *The National Enterprise Board*, published March 1973 included proposals to give a Labour government powers to impose compulsory planning agreements. Between 20 and 25 of the largest 100 manufacturing companies accounting for around one-third of manufacturing output were to be nationalised with or without the consent of their boards of directors. This paper was approved at the 1973 Labour Party conference.

This radical leftward shift in industrial policy was primarily a result of the working class growing far more militant under the Heath government. The Labour leadership learned that, even if it could fully determine party policy, it would have difficulty winning the next election on a warmed-up version of its previous manifesto.

Industrial militancy forced Heath to abandon the 'Selsdon Man' strategy of the 1970–72 period. His policies then became broadly indistinguishable from those the 1964–70 Labour government imposed in its latter days – statutory incomes policies, helping firms in difficulty, and so on. After 1972 Wilson had to find new policies to avoid being taken for a Tory.

Working-class militants had gone on fighting against the Tories after Heath had borrowed Wilson-style policies and had brought down the government. They had demonstrated clearly that they were in no mood to accept such measures from either party.

Finally, militants campaigned actively in the constituencies and trade unions to change Labour policy and supported those in the Parliamentary Party and on the executive who sought to do likewise. The shift in the political balance of motions discussed at Labour Party and trade union conferences shows this development, as does an enormous growth in support for Tony Benn throughout the Labour movement. It was Benn, in his capacity as Labour Party chairperson, who established in 1972 the policy-formulating executive sub-committees which drew up the new programme.

The February 1974 Manifesto

The Labour left's gain in strength during opposition was reflected in the programme on which Labour fought the February 1974 election. It had two basic strands. First, there was to be a major redistribution of income, wealth and social service provision in favour of the working class and the relatively worse-off. Secondly, capital's control over economic activity was to be substantially reduced.

On the redistribution front, the manifesto pledged the party to 'achieve far greater economic equality – in income, wealth and living standards', to 'increase social equality by giving far greater importance to full employment, housing, education and social benefits' and to 'eliminate poverty wherever it exists in Britain'. Among the specific measures promised were:

- an immediate increase in pensions and future rises in line with average annual earnings;
- an increase in child allowances;
- the introduction of food subsidies;
- the repeal of the Housing Finance Act and the introduction of rent control;
- the introduction of an annual wealth tax;
- the abolition of prescription charges and the phasing out of pay beds in the NHS;
- the expansion of education provision and the introduction of a national nursery school scheme.

In the field of economic activity, the manifesto reiterated the main lines of Labour's 1972–74 strategy. On nationalisation it stated that Labour would 'not confine the extension of the public sector to loss-making and subsidised industries' but would 'also take over profitable sections or individual firms in those industries where a public holding is essential to enable the government to control prices, stimulate investment, encourage exports, create employment, protect workers and consumers from the activities of irresponsible multi-national companies, and to plan the national economy in the national interest' and that it would 'create a powerful National Enterprise Board with the structure and functions set out in *Labour's Programme 1973*'. Specific commitments on public ownership included:

- the nationalisation of shipbuilding, ship-repairing and marine engineering, ports and the manufacture of airframes and aero-engines:

- the take-over of sections of pharmaceuticals, road haulage, construction and machine tools;
- the return to public ownership of all assets and licences hived off by the Heath government;
- full public ownership of all North Sea and Celtic Sea oil and gas resources and majority public participation in and 'full government control' of the extraction and distribution of these resources;
- the taking into common ownership of land required for development and of mineral rights.

There was no specific reference in the manifesto to a National Enterprise Board takeover of 20–25 companies. It was also unclear whether planning agreements were to be compulsory. But the programme nevertheless implied a major extension of state control over profitable private industry through nationalisation and government direction.

This was the most important way in which Labour pledged itself to reduce economic control by private capital. But it was not the only one. The manifesto also committed the party to increasing worker and trade union control over economic activity. This objective was to be pursued on a number of fronts.

Firstly, the rights of shareholders and managers to control their companies' operations were to be restricted by requiring them to include workers' representatives on certain decision-making bodies. Labour pledged itself to introduce an Industrial Democracy Act along lines 'agreed in our discussions with the TUC'.

The principles were later spelled out in *Labour's Programme for Britain 1976*, which stated that all companies employing over 2,000 workers were to be required by law to establish a Main Policy Board, half the places on which 'would be available for workers' representatives, elected through the recognised trade union machinery'.

Secondly, companies' decision-making powers with regard to employment were to be curtailed by law. Labour promised to introduce an Employment Protection Act.

Thirdly, certain legal restrictions on trade unions were to be removed. The repeal of anti-trade union legislation would strengthen the unions and allow them to exert greater influence over economic decisions. Labour pledged itself to repeal the Industrial Relations Act, to abolish the Pay Board and to end statutory incomes policy.

Finally, Labour proposed to increase TUC influence over national economic and social policy through a 'Social Contract'. The origin of the Social Contract was a 1973 TUC-Labour Party liaison committee document entitled *Economic Policy and the Cost of Living.* This short and vague statement wrote of the need for 'an alternative strategy to fight inflation . . . to provide the basis for co-operation between the trade unions and the [forthcoming Labour] government'. It included a number of specific policy commitments on Labour's behalf (all of which were later included in the February 1974 election manifesto). The TUC, for its part, agreed to help 'create the right economic climate for money incomes to grow in line with production'.

Labour's two basic policy thrusts, redistribution and reduced control by capital over production, were summed up in the manifesto as the intention to 'bring about a fundamental and irreversible shift in the balance of power and wealth in favour of working people and their families'.

The 1974 programme, which, with various additions and amendments, has come to be known as the Alternative Economic Strategy and to be associated primarily with Benn, the Tribunites, the TUC and the Communist Party, does not, in our view, constitute a viable strategy for socialism. (This position is argued at length in Chapter 5 below.) But this does not mean the strategy is just another version of Tory economic policies or of previous and subsequent Labour ones.

It may not be a viable strategy for socialism, but it is anti-capitalist. Its redistributional proposals are quite inimical to the interests of capital. Its proposals for increased state and trade union control over profitable manufacturing industry are a direct threat to the economic power of the capitalist class. If fully and successfully implemented, the strategy would severely curtail capital's control of economic activity.

This is why it was and is violently opposed by the CBI and

representatives of international capital, who view it as a major threat to the stability of the system. William Rogers, a high ranking official in the US State Department involved in negotiations over the December 1976 International Monetary Fund loan to the UK, described the US authorities' assessment of the situation as follows:

> We all had the feeling it could come apart in quite a serious way. As I saw it, it was a choice between Britain remaining in the liberal financial system of the West as opposed to a radical change of course because we were concerned about Tony Benn precipitating a policy decision by Britain to turn its back on the IMF. I think if that had happened the whole system would have begun to come apart. God knows what Italy might have done; then France might have taken a radical change in the same direction. It would not only have had consequences for the economic recovery, it would have had great political consequences. So we tended to see it in cosmic terms. (quoted *Sunday Times*, 21 May 1978)

The composition of the new government

The composition of the new Parliamentary Labour Party and government had also shifted significantly leftwards. Wilson's old leadership had survived the radicalisation at the base of the party during opposition, but had been unable to prevent this process from influencing the composition of the Parliamentary Party itself.

The most direct way in which the constituency parties were able to affect the political complexion of the Parliamentary Party was through candidate selection. And so they did. Of the 50 new Labour MPs elected in February, 28 immediately joined the Tribune group, bringing its total membership to 68.

Pressure from the trade unions, the constituency parties and the parliamentary party, also influenced Wilson's cabinet appointments. A number of prominent left-wingers were given posts. The most important appointments were those of Michael Foot (still regarded at the time as a left-winger) to the Department of Employment, and of Benn to the Department of Industry.

Back to work with Labour

Labour's immediate objective was a settlement with the miners.

The Pay Board report on the National Union of Mineworkers, commissioned by Whitelaw, was available when Wilson took office. It recommended 'exceptional' payments. Labour settled with increases ranging from 22–32 per cent. Industry was back to five-day working within a week of the election. With the immediate industrial and parliamentary political crisis thus defused, Labour could start keeping its manifesto promises.

Early redistributional measures

During its early months in office, Labour implemented a substantial number of the redistributional measures it had pledged. Healey's first Budget, on 26 March 1974, included some good news for the less well-off. Pensions were raised as promised. Food subsidies were increased by £500m for the financial year 1974–75 and rent subsidies by £70m. Local authorities were encouraged to increase council house building. The Housing Finance Act was abolished and a rent freeze imposed.

At the other end of the spectrum, the tax burden was increased for capital and the rich. Corporation tax was raised, and its payment required more promptly. Income tax was raised disproportionately for the recipients of high salaries and unearned income. Gift and wealth taxes were introduced and the system of tax relief on personal borrowing interest payments introduced by Barber was abolished. A second budget on 22 July 1974 contained further measures to benefit those on low incomes. Housing subsidies were increased and the standard rate of VAT was cut from 10 to 8 per cent.

The general approach to pay, prices and the unions also favoured the organised working class against capital in the short-term struggle over wages (see below).

Industrial policy

Benn, assisted by his deputy, leading Tribunite Eric Heffer, immediately began to draft a White Paper to form the basis for a new Industry Act. Benn's proposals were supported by the National Executive Committee and the Tribunites, but violently opposed by Wilson, Healey and the Civil Service. The paper reportedly went through no less than 25 drafts. The final result was a victory for the right wing (see below).

Pending internal agreement on new legislation, Labour operated under the terms of the Tories' Industry Act. Money was made available to modernise a few specific industries (wool textiles, foundries, machine tools and printing machinery) and for certain investment projects within other industries. During winter 1974–75, the Department of Industry gave assistance to a number of firms in immediate difficulties.

In six of the latter cases (including three workers' co-operatives: Scottish Daily News, Triumph-Meriden and Kirkby Manufacturing.) Benn gave assistance against the recommendation of the Industrial Development Advisory Board, whose function under the 1972 Act was to advise on the commercial viability of investment projects.

Support for the three co-operatives had an important symbolic value. But, in terms of real economic effects, Labour's early industrial policy differed only marginally from that pursued towards the end of the Heath era. The new Labour government implemented few of its pledges to transfer elements of control over production from capital to the state.

Trade unions, pay and prices

The government lost no time undoing Tory legal restraints on unions. It repealed the Industrial Relations Act, abolished the Pay Board and abandoned Heath's statutory incomes policy.

The Parliamentary Party's commitment to free collective bargaining, albeit within the context of the vaguely delineated Social Contract, was extremely strong at this time. In the words of one observer: 'A statutory incomes policy – indeed any interference with collective bargaining – was out. Even to mention it in Labour circles in 1974 was like using a four-letter word in a nineteenth century drawing-room.' (Stewart, p. 191).

A new Department of Prices and Consumer Protection was created and the system of price controls inherited from the Tories was extended and tightened. This move went some way towards the TUC-Labour Party liaison committee's demand in *Economic Policy and the Cost of Living* for 'a permanent system of price controls' to 'prevent the erosion of real wages'.

In sum, then, Labour kept election promises on the redistributional and industrial relations fronts in a fairly rapid and resolute manner. But its activity in these spheres contrasts sharply with its lack of it in the field of state control over industry. There the government made almost no moves to implement the industrial policy outlined in its manifesto.

The context of early Labour policy

Before assessing the effects of Labour's policies and analysing developments during the early months of the Labour government, it may be helpful to recapitulate the main features of the situation Labour had inherited.

Developments in the world economy were dominated by the oil crisis. When the oil price rises were imposed in winter 1973–74, world-capitalist output was already decelerating sharply as a result of restrictive demand-management policies imposed in the wake of the inflationary and speculative miniboom of 1972–73. The increase in oil prices diverted funds into the hands of OPEC members who were unable to spend them immediately. This caused the conditions for realising surplus value to deteriorate still further. The sharp rise in fuel costs gave inflation a fillip, which prompted a further round of restrictive monetary and fiscal policies. Output collapsed in the summer of 1974. Over the next nine months world-capitalist industrial production fell by 10 per cent, unemployment rose by some 10m and inflation decelerated from 15 to 10 per cent. So much for the international economic climate.

At home, almost every economic indicator had worsened considerably under the Tories. By 1973 the post-tax rate of profit had fallen to 5.7 per cent and the share of world manufacturing exports to 9.4 per cent, despite a rapid depreciation of sterling. The rate of accumulation in manufacturing was only half the EEC average and one-sixth of that in Japan. The balance of payments was in deficit to the tune of £1bn and inflation had risen to 9.1 per cent for the year.

And things were getting worse by the time of the February election. Output had failed to grow during the last nine months of

1973 and the OECD was predicting a fall of 2.5 per cent during 1974. By the end of 1973, the balance of payments deficit was running at an annual rate of £2.5bn and it was estimated that the oil price rise would add a further £1bn to it. The rate of inflation was also rising sharply. Prices rose by 12¾ per cent between January 1973 and January 1974. Between July 1973 and January 1974, they rose at an annual rate of 19 per cent. The CBI industrial trends survey for January 1974 showed the lowest level of business confidence ever in its 16 years.

Finally, Labour faced a militant, organised working class with high expectations.

Developments during Labour's early months

The most important broad trends during the early months of Labour rule were predictable, given their policies and the context. Class confrontation in the factories cooled down, the political situation stabilised and economic performance deteriorated significantly.

Crucial to all three developments was the pace of wage rises, up from an annual rate of 12.5 per cent at the end of 1973 to 25.4 per cent at the end of 1974.

Better pay deals were only to be expected. Labour had come to power because the miners had defeated Heath. Its electoral support came from militants who expected concessions and from voters who accepted Labour's claim that, unlike the Tories, it would win the unions' co-operation. But it was a minority government, and would clearly need further electoral support in the near future. It was also waiting for the TUC Conference to ratify the Social Contract. In the circumstances it is hardly surprising that the government made abundantly clear in both word and deed that it was not prepared to launch or assist in a confrontation with the unions.

Capitalists rightly felt they were in a relatively weak position. A tough response to pay demands could, they knew, prompt demands for more active government intervention in the private sector. They assessed the balance of forces as unfavourable and yielded over pay, thus diluting class confrontation on the industrial front.

Legal restraints on trade unions had been eased and Healey had fulfilled his pledge to divert funds to the less well-off. These measures, the relatively left complexion of the government and the fact that earnings were keeping comfortably ahead of prices all helped to consolidate militants' support for Labour. The electorate had seen a rapid return to a five-day week. Industrial confrontation had simmered down and the TUC Conference had endorsed the Social Contract in September 1974. Many non-militant voters were satisfied Labour had justified its claim to obtain the unions' co-operation. The government thus won a small overall majority in a General Election on 10 October 1974.

But this relative stabilisation on the industrial and political fronts was achieved only at the expense of more deterioration in economic performance. The economic crisis bit deeper during 1974 and spring 1975.

The oil price rise, and the boom in international commodity prices which followed it, increased costs. The conditions for producing surplus value grew worse. Firms in the UK had to face an extra cost burden because wages went up faster than abroad. So conditions for producing surplus value not only got worse, but also deteriorated relative to those abroad, giving a further twist to the long-term decline of UK competitiveness.

OPEC was hanging on to some $1\frac{1}{2}$ per cent of world purchasing power, aggravating the conditions metropolitan capital faced for realisation. Then most major economies implemented deflationary policies in the spring and summer of 1974, making prospects even more gloomy. The UK was, however, an exception. Healey's budgets were more or less neutral with respect to total expenditure. So although conditions for realisation deteriorated absolutely in the UK, they did so to a smaller extent than elsewhere.

The net outcome was disastrous for UK capital. Because the conditions for producing surplus value and those for realising it both deteriorated simultaneously, profitability slid down again. The pre-tax rate of profit fell from 7.2 per cent in 1973 to 4.0 per cent in 1974. The post-tax situation deteriorated even more sharply because of tighter company taxation introduced in the March 1974 Budget. On the basis of the tax liabilities and investment allowances operative until November 1974 (see below on the November changes), the post-tax rate of profit fell from 3.4 per cent in 1973 to *minus* 0.3 per cent in 1974.

Many companies whose profitability had declined and who were required to pay corporation tax more promptly from the March budget went deeper into debt. The company-sector increased its rate of borrowing around £200m a quarter in the summer of 1973 to about £1400m in the summer of 1974.

Because realisation conditions held up better in the UK than elsewhere, profits, output and employment did not feel the impact of soaring costs and deteriorating conditions for producing surplus value quite so soon as in other countries.

But this cushioning of UK capital relative to its competitors had contradictory effects. The immediate benefits were obtained only at the cost of intensifying the underlying problem of competitiveness. If realisation conditions had deteriorated as sharply in the UK as elsewhere in 1974, then either inflation and/or output and employment levels would have fallen. Either would have eased the deterioration in conditions for producing surplus value which was destroying UK competitiveness.

More unemployment would have weakened workers' bargaining power and reduced the rate at which wage costs grew. If prices had gone up less steeply, wage demands would have been more moderate since the extra pay needed merely to offset inflation would have been less. Thus, if realisation conditions had not held up as well as they did, then the wage/price spiral would have been less steep and UK competitiveness would have deteriorated less rapidly.

By early 1975 – to allow the narrative of economic developments to run ahead of that of policy for a moment – this spiral had become very steep indeed, with both earnings and prices rising by around 25 per cent a year.

The move to the right

The deterioration in UK competitiveness undoubtedly contributed to the about-face in government policy heralded in Denis Healey's Budget speech, delivered only days after the October election. The speech amounted to a complete reversal of Labour's strategic economic objectives.

The previous policy of redistributing money towards low income groups was replaced by one of directing it back towards capital. The policy of reducing capital's control over production gave way to one of seeking an economic climate within which companies would find it worth while to invest.

These two reversals were, of course, related. Once the government gave up the idea of curbing capital's economic power, it had to gear distributional policies to companies' needs if investment was to take place. Low profitability implies redistribution away from workers towards capital. As Healey later put it: 'Firms will only expand and invest if they can see scope for making profits.'

The capitalist class, badly placed to resist wage demands, subjected the government to intense pressure to abandon its election policies. The *Financial Times* (16 October 1974) reported that 'the CBI told Mr Wilson that there was absolutely no room for compromise or negotiation about further state intervention in industry and further nationalisation'. Two days before the Budget, the Director of the CBI had sent Wilson an open letter, arguing that 'price control, profit limitations and socialist threats would ensure that the economic crisis . . . could bring the country down within a year'. On the Monday after the election Pilkingtons announced that their £150m investment programme would be shelved 'until such time as essential changes are made in taxation and price control' – a blatant threat of a 'strike of capital'.

The change in policies implemented was less sharp than that in official pronouncements. Most of the Labour leadership had never subscribed to much of the February 1974 position, and had prevented implementation of any important element of the alternative industrial strategy before the announcement of policy reversal in November 1974. Moreover, they were compelled to tread warily for some months more. Redistribution policies were reversed only gradually.

The November Budget was nevertheless a watershed. It marked the beginning of a period of systematic, if jerky, movement to the right as the Wilson-Healey-Callaghan trio became increasingly able to push through anti-working class measures.

The most important Budget measures to divert income to capital were:

- reduction of corporation tax liability on stock appreciation;
- slacker price controls, allowing companies to pass on in price rises 80 per cent of increases in labour costs and 17½ per cent of the cost of fixed investment.

In addition, £1bn of loans were to be made available to companies over two years for investment through Finance For Industry.

It was estimated that the total financial benefits to companies would be around £1.5bn in 1975. The post-tax rate of profit for 1974 calculated on the basis of the post-November tax structure was 4.1 per cent, as opposed to minus 0.3 per cent on the basis of the pre-November structure. The easing of the price code would, it was estimated, raise profits in 1975 by £800m and the rate of inflation by 1 percentage point.

Ominously, Healey announced restricted growth of public expenditure – to 2 per cent a year for the next four years – and estimated that unemployment would continue to rise (though remaining below a million). He warned that if pay claims were not restricted to levels compatible with the TUC guidelines, he would deflate the economy.

The most plausible interpretation of the thinking behind the November Budget runs as follows. The Labour leadership was aware of the dire situation facing UK capital, wanted to improve things and to reverse the pressures which caused the problem. The October election victory meant that Labour was relatively secure in office, making possible redistributional measures to ease capital's plight which would be unpopular with its supporters.

Wilson and company were aware that such diversion of income was only a stop-gap measure. If the underlying determinants of international competitiveness could not be improved, UK capital would continue to experience severe difficulties. The most important factor worsening international competitiveness at the time was the severe wage/price spiral. But the strength and influence of militants within trade unions and constituencies, and of their supporters within the Parliamentary Party, was such that Wilson and Healey did not feel able to take decisive action on the wages front. Exhortation and vague threats were, they felt, the most that was politically possible.

The TUC guidelines on pay, to which Healey referred in his budget speech, were published by the government in December. They were extremely vague. Within the next few months, as both wages and prices continued to escalate, settlement of 25–30 per cent for nurses, teachers, bakers and local authority workers were publicly defended by both the TUC and the government as being within the terms of the social contract.

The April 1975 Budget was mildly deflationary, intended to cut total demand for the remainder of the year by £330m. Income tax was raised by two percentage points (but allowances were also raised so that one-third of workers paid no extra tax). Excise duties were raised and the top VAT rate of 25 per cent, previously applicable only to petrol, was extended to a wide range of 'luxury' items. Public expenditure plans for 1976–77 were cut by £900m.

Given the situation on the wages and prices front, it was, from the point of view of capital's economic needs, too little too late. But the trade union leadership's low-key response to Healey's Budget speech announcement that unemployment was expected shortly to reach the psychologically significant figure of one million gave some indication of the increasing ease with which the Labour leadership could impose anti-working class policies.

Two events in the spring and summer of 1975 weakened and isolated militants and the left of the Labour Party. The Wilson-Healey leadership took advantage of them to shift government economic policy more decisively to the right.

The first event was the defeat of the left in a referendum on EEC membership. Labour's February 1974 manifesto had promised that Labour would undertake 'a fundamental renegotiation' of Britain's membership terms which would be put before the electorate for approval by either a referendum or a General Election. After Callaghan had (fractionally) renegotiated the terms, a referendum was fixed for 5 June 1975.

Broadly speaking, the right of the Labour Party was in favour of the new terms and the left wanted rejection and withdrawal from the EEC. During the pre-referendum campaign period, the principle of collective responsibility was waived and individual members of the government were free to argue for either position. The right won a resounding victory, as 67.2 per cent of those voting supported acceptance.

The left suffered a major public defeat. It had failed to provide a convincing alternative to right-wing arguments in favour of EEC membership. Wilson seized the opportunity to demote Benn from the Department of Industry to Energy. Since negotiation with oil companies over the terms of participation in North Sea oil was at first explicitly excluded from his brief, this reduced Benn's power considerably.

The second event which strengthened the right was the sterling crisis of June 1975. The UK balance of payments had been heavily in deficit for some time. The effective sterling exchange rate (the value of the pound measured against a weighted average of other currencies) had, by the first quarter of 1975, fallen by 29 per cent since December 1971. UK competitiveness was sinking fast by the spring of 1975. Retail prices rose at an annual rate of nearly 38 per cent in the second quarter compared with an average of some 10 per cent for the UK's major competitors. Wage settlements of 30 per cent or so were still common and in the second quarter of 1975 average earnings were 27 per cent higher than in the previous year, auguring continued high rates of inflation. Sterling was hardly the ideal currency in which to hold money.

The pound fell 4 per cent in the six weeks to mid-June. On 21 June, Healey said that the UK had to demonstrate to the world that it could reduce inflation to single figures by the end of 1976. He did not say how. 'The world' was unimpressed. Pressure on sterling intensified and on 30 June the pound fell by 1.3 per cent in a single trading session.

The following day, Healey announced that the government would reduce inflation to an annual rate of 10 per cent by the end of the next pay round and to single figures by the end of 1976. Wage increases were to be restricted to 10 per cent in the following round. This restriction was, if possible, to be achieved by voluntary agreement with the TUC. Otherwise a statutory limit would be imposed.

They got almost instant agreement. Within the next ten days both the government and the TUC published guidelines for 'voluntary income restraint'. The two documents were almost identical in essentials; there was to be a £6 limit on all settlements made prior to 1 August 1976.

The TUC leadership's acceptance of the £6 limit was the government's first real gain from the Social Contract. And it was a major one. Union leaders had agreed to help the government impose cuts on their members – with inflation running at some 30 per cent it was perfectly plain that a £6 limit implied a fall in real earnings. The TUC leadership set no conditions on the agreement.

The deal over, the £6 limit set the tone for all but the last few months of Labour's rule. The next few years were to be characterised by successful co-operation between the TUC and parliamentary party leaderships on implementation of directly anti-working-class policies.

How they got away with it

A few months before that, most observers would have judged the prospects of the TUC accepting voluntary pay restraint to be low. They would have argued that, however much the TUC leadership might have wanted the deal, it would not have been on. Militants' strength would have prevented rank and file acceptance. Yet in the summer of 1975 the TUC did the deal on the £6 limit without arousing mass opposition. How come?

One explanation favoured by sections of the left is that the TUC and parliamentary party leaderships were able to implement anti-working-class policies only by acting in an increasingly undemocratic manner – by intervening in local trade union branches, trades councils and constituency parties to impose policies opposed at local level and by ignoring mandates laid down by annual conferences.

But if undemocratic procedures are to be forced through successfully, there has to be a certain balance of forces. If militants had been as strong at this time as they had been before Labour took power, attempts to operate undemocratically would undoubtedly have encountered fiercer opposition from the membership.

There is, in fact, considerable evidence that many of the more important measures were supported by a majority of the rank and file. The £6 limit won a majority at both TUC and Labour Party annual conferences. The 1976–77 policy of modest tax cuts made conditional on the observance of a 5 per cent ceiling on settlements received even larger majorities at both conferences.

The fact is that militants' self-confidence and influence had weakened considerably by the summer of 1975. The heyday of industrial militancy had proved action could win gains for the movement. Under the Tories, direct action had shelved anti-trade-union legislation and thrown out a nakedly anti-working-class government. In the early months of Labour's rule it had brought substantial increases in real earnings. But by spring 1975 many workers felt the heyday was over.

Prices had by that time caught up with wages. Many workers believed it was necessary under free collective bargaining to go on demanding increases to protect living standards against future inflation, but that the collective bargaining system had become a liability to the labour movement. It had been essential, they reasoned, to have a system through which to fight for large pay rises while inflation had been due to factors outside their control, such as import prices. This, they believed, had been the case in 1972–73. But once wage rises themselves became chiefly responsible for inflation, one important effect of a steep wage/price spiral was, by spring 1975, to damage UK competitiveness and increase unemployment.

This line of thinking was common and many militants were influenced by it. They truly believed wage-generated inflation was damaging the UK economy and thereby preventing the government from carrying out policies in favour of the working class. In other words, there was considerable grass-roots support for the Social Contract.

This support was reinforced by the June sterling crisis. 'International speculators' had long been Harold Wilson's favourite villains and the Labour leadership seized the opportunity to depict the situation as one in which its hands were tied by wicked gnomes.

Political activists could have countered this mood and won support for active opposition to pay restraint if there had been a convincing alternative. To qualify, it would have had to appear viable in principle – that is, based on a programme to protect jobs and living standards without exacerbating the underlying problems and yielding even greater difficulties – and winnable in practice.

The main alternative in 1975 was the Alternative Economic

Strategy and its most influential advocates Benn and the Tribunites. The way they presented the strategy ensured activists would not be able to fight for it successfully.

While in opposition, Benn had argued that the strategy should be seen as a solution to the crisis rather than as a programme to be implemented after it had been resolved. For example, he said at the 1973 Labour Party conference that 'the crisis that we inherit when we come to power will be the occasion for fundamental change and not the excuse for postponing it'.

At the time of the June 1975 sterling crisis, the Labour leadership (which did not support the strategy anyway) argued that economic difficulties made it necessary to postpone manifesto policies and to impose anti-working class measures temporarily. In other words, the strategy was a luxury that they could afford only after the crisis had been resolved.

Neither Benn nor the Tribunites fought effectively against this line. Indeed, it seems Benn did not even argue the case within the Parliamentary Party leadership. The first occasion on which he argued in full cabinet that anti-working-class policies should be abandoned and the strategy implemented immediately was in the summer of 1976 (*Sunday Times*, May 21 1978). So it is hardly surprising that rank and file political activists found difficulty presenting the strategy as an immediate practical alternative to wage restraint.

And how would the strategy have been carried out? It had consistently been presented as a programme to be enacted by parliament. Its implementation had always been conditional on the election of a left-Labour government which would implement the programme 'from the top downward' by legislative means.

The fact that the strategy had been sold in this way guaranteed difficulties however its leading advocates reacted in the summer of 1975. If Benn and the Tribunites had tried to lead a grass-roots revolt against the government's move to the right then they would have had to shift position on the way the strategy was to be fought for, stressing industrial action for the first time. But they continued to talk of the strategy in purely parliamentary terms, even though it was clear they had been defeated in the parliamentary arena. They made no move to campaign at trade union and Labour Party meetings up and down the country for direct action against wage cuts and in favour of alternative policies.

To our knowledge, neither Benn nor any leading Tribunite has ever offered any justification or self-criticism for this capitulation.

The successful imposition of the £6 limit is in many ways the obvious point at which to end this account of Labour's scramble to the right. The period from the summer of 1975 through to the strike wave in the winter of 1978–79 was an endless, dismal parade of successfully imposed anti-working class measures, which apparently did little to check the head-long decline of UK capital or to stimulate a genuine socialist alternative to reformism. But it is worth examining the International Monetary Fund loan of December 1976, if only because many Labour supporters believe that the conditions attached were the most important factor preventing the party implementing its programme.

The IMF loan

Early in 1976, the Bank of England decided to engineer a devaluation of the pound. The idea was to improve UK competitiveness, by reducing the price of UK exports and increasing that of imports, and hence give a boost to industry. With the system of floating exchange rates then operating, devaluation could not be achieved at a stroke. The pound would have to float down gently over a few weeks. Such a policy was risky. If it became known, or suspected, that the Bank was engineering a fall, an uncontrollable run on sterling might begin.

The Bank hoped to avoid this by keeping its policy secret. But its attempts to nudge the pound down misfired when the market mistakenly concluded that the UK was intentionally selling while the pound was falling. Selling your own currency while it is depreciating is to international banking what dealing off the bottom of the pack is to poker. Americans with a different taste in party games call it 'dirty pool'.

The market panicked. The pound fell through the $2.00 barrier for the first time. Within a week it was down to $1.90, about the level the Bank desired. But it did not stop there. It continued down through the $1.80s and into the $1.70s.

On Friday 4 June, with the pound at $1.71 and still falling, a $5bn 'standby' loan for the UK was arranged by foreign Central Banks. Such loans are normally extended until confidence in the currency is restored. But the Americans told Healey and Callaghan that this one would under no circumstances continue beyond six months. The purpose of the deadline was quite straightforward: to force the UK to approach the IMF for a loan to repay what it had spent of its borrowings.

Arthur Burns, Chairman of the US Federal Reserve Bank, described the American attitude as follows:

> I had my doubts whether the British could correct the fault in their economic management on their own. You must remember I am a neanderthal conservative, and naturally suspicious of a Labour government. I thought it was a profligate government. (*Sunday Times*, 28 May 1978)

They knew that the IMF, which was US-dominated and heavily 'monetarist', thought likewise and would make a loan to the UK conditional on massive spending cuts. The standby loan was the IMF's fish-bait to hook the wayward UK.

By 9 September, $1½bn of the standby had been spent. Healey instructed the Bank to pull out and stop supporting the pound. During the first two days of the Labour Party conference, sterling fell by 7½ per cent, conveniently weakening opposition to an IMF loan. Healey then announced the government would apply.

Healey offered the IMF a package it accepted featuring a $3bn reduction in the public sector borrowing requirement (excess of government expenditure over revenue) over two years, to be achieved mainly by cuts in government expenditure, in return for a loan. Cabinet opposition to the terms collapsed, as did a proposal to reject them and impose import controls. The left not only voted for acceptance of the IMF terms but also 'became the most influential proselytisers for the package' (*Sunday Times*, 28 May 1978). As one of them put it: 'We said to the Tribune Group, you are just going to have to close your eyes and walk backwards into the lobby.' Hardly a recipe for clear-sighted politics.

How is the IMF's role to be evaluated? Were the IMF and its US backers the real villains of the piece? Or were they merely convenient fallguys for Callaghan? There is truth in both views.

Neither the US nor the IMF created the sterling crisis or the underlying difficulties which prompted it. Nor did they intensify them. Any government seriously attempting to resolve the crisis in capital's interests – a project to which the Labour leadership was firmly committed by the time of the IMF loan – would at some point have been compelled by events to adopt policies similar to those imposed by the IMF. There is thus an important sense in which the IMF functioned as a fallguy (bad and foreign), to be blamed by the government for policies which British capital was itself demanding.

As Fred Hirsch, a former IMF official, explained in the *Guardian*:

> There has been a persistent tendency, originating in the City and transmitted through the financial press, to overstate the independent influence of external finance [i.e. the IMF] and to understate the extent to which this serves as a cover or front for domestic . . . interest groups. The external card is the joker in their pack and it is hardly surprising that they play it.

But Callaghan and Healey would not have imposed such large cuts at the time had the IMF not insisted. They were reluctant to do so largely because they were afraid the move would be politically unacceptable. They feared a revolt within the parliamentary party, a general election and defeat. The IMF was therefore directly responsible for the scale and timing of the spring 1977 round of cuts.

But no revolt occurred. Benn and the Tribunites failed to campaign against the leadership's argument that its hands were tied by the IMF. So Healey and Callaghan gained confidence in their ability to impose anti-working class measures and continued to do so after the IMF ceased to exert an influence.

Labour's economic record

Burying the alternative industrial strategy

The August 1974 White Paper *The Regeneration of British Industry* had retained the principle of the taking over of profitable manufacturing companies. 'The National Enterprise Board will be the instrument by which the government ensures that the nation's resources are deployed to the benefit of all, by extending public ownership into profitable manufacturing industry.' But the powers envisaged for the board were very severely weakened by the inclusion of the clause 'holdings in companies . . . should be acquired by agreement'.

The government was slow to transform the White Paper proposals into legislation. There were delaying tactics in the House of Lords and further concessions on content. The Act was eventually passed in November 1975. By this time, super-tycoon Ryder had been appointed industrial advisor to the government and chairperson-designate of the board. Draft guidelines for the National Enterprise Board's operation were not published until March 1976.

The 1975 act specified that the board's borrowing was not to exceed £1000m over a five-year period. The board would have to bid for shares in the open market unless the directors of a company it wished to take over agreed to the move, hardly likely unless the company was effectively bankrupt. These two provisions were sufficient to prevent the National Enterprise Board acquiring profitable companies to any significant extent. The £1000m was insufficient to buy, say, ICI at prevailing share prices and, given inevitable opposition to any board purchase from directors, the City and the CBI, it became very unlikely that the board would be able to persuade shareholders in a profitable company to sell out.

Eight companies already under public ownership – mostly acquired under the terms of the 1972 Industry Act because they were on the edge of bankruptcy – were transferred to the board. National Enterprise Board operations were from the beginning almost entirely restricted to dealings with these companies. Two of them (British Leyland and Rolls Royce) accounted between them for nine-tenths of the board's operation in the first six months of 1978.

The board's policy towards these companies was to press through savage reductions in operating levels in an attempt to restore them to commercial viability. In 1976 and 1977 19,000 jobs were lost at British Leyland, 5,600 at Rolls Royce, 1,100 at Ferranti, 800 at Alfred Herbert and 1,300 at International Computers.

The main move on 'industrial democracy' was the initially

successful attempt to involve the trade unions in participation exercises at BL, the object of which was to secure their agreement for rationalisation.

The other activities of the board were largely peripheral and of a purely commercial nature. They consisted mainly of making loans at commercial rates to small and medium-sized companies. Neither banking or other capital had significant objections to this.

So much for the National Enterprise Board, an institution which Wilson had described, apparently with a straight face, as 'the greatest leap forward in economic thinking and policy since John Maynard Keynes' (quoted Holland, p. 152).

The original planning agreement proposals fared no better. By the time of the August 1975 White Paper, the idea of making them compulsory had been dropped. And companies were hardly going to volunteer them. As one put it: 'We would sign a planning agreement tomorrow if we could do it our way . . . we are not reassured by the way in which the government sees planning agreements and so we will not sign one' (quoted in *The Times*, 17 February 1977).

Only one so-called planning agreement has ever been signed, with Chrysler UK in the spring of 1976. It was reached as part of a £162.5m bailing-out operation, and was an economically meaningless device to help the government save face.

Having effectively abandoned the 1972–74 industrial strategy in this way, in November 1975 the government presented the National Economic Development Council with a set of proposals for an alternative long-term industrial strategy. Three types of manufacturing sectors were to be selected for treatment: ones which were intrinsically successful, ones which could be successful if appropriate action were taken and ones which did not fall into either of the first two categories, but were important for the rest of industry, for example, component suppliers.

About two-thirds of manufacturing was placed within one or other of these categories. The implication was that the remaining third should be allowed to go to the wall. Tripartite NEDC sector working parties representing employers, unions and government, were to be set up for the 40 or so sectors placed within these categories.

The working parties served two main functions. First, they

provided a forum within which capital could formally negotiate with the government (and to a lesser extent the unions) over the allocation among sectors and firms of the £3000m or so the state handed out to industry every year. Secondly, they made possible a more rapid and orderly rationalisation of certain industries. They brought about scrapping of old plant by a process of agreement and compensation rather than one of cut-throat competition and bankruptcy. Planned rationalisation inevitably involved job loss. As the *TUC Economic Review* lamely noted: 'implicit in some of the working party reports is the idea that employment reductions are needed.'

The lengths to which Labour was prepared to go to avoid implementing its industrial policy is well illustrated by the Chrysler affair. When the American Chrysler Corporation wanted to pull out of its loss-making subsidiary Chrysler UK, it offered the government £35m to take the company off its hands, thereby hoping to avoid redundancy pay and other costs of closure. The government was not prepared to see the company close down, with a direct loss of 25,000 jobs and the indirect loss of another 30,000 at least. But it was also unwilling to nationalise Chrysler and integrate it with BL.

Eventually the government provided a £55m loan for investment and guaranteed to cover a proportion of losses incurred between 1976 and 1979 up to a total of £72.5m. Rationalisation involving the loss of 8,200 direct jobs was agreed. In return for this support, Chrysler UK magnanimously agreed to sign a planning agreement. It was so meaningless that later Chrysler Europe, including Chrysler UK, was taken over by Peugeot without the Labour government even being informed in advance.

The social contract and living standards

Having abandoned manifesto commitments to reduce capital's sway over economic activity, Labour was, given the crisis, inevitably drawn into a programme of systematic attacks on jobs and living standards in an attempt to restore profitability and competitiveness. This section charts the effects of its policies on working-class living standards.

The movement of real take-home pay is shown below between dates corresponding to successive periods of pay policy (Table 1).

1: Wages, Prices and Real Pay: UK, 1974–79

	Cost of living	Earnings	Level of take-home pay
	Percentage increase on previous year		Index (April 1974 = 100)
July 1974	17.1	18.1	105
July 1975	26.3	27.7	101
July 1976	12.9	13.9	103
July 1977	17.6	8.9	97
July 1978	7.8	14.2	104
March 1979	9.8	14.9	105

Source: Labour Research, *various issues.*

Real earnings rose rapidly in the early months of Labour rule as Heath's Phase III was abandoned and money wages surged ahead of prices. Between April and December 1974 real earnings grew by 8 per cent. By the spring of 1975, however, prices had accelerated rapidly, and overtaken wages. Real take-home pay had begun to fall. By June 1975 it was 9 per cent down on the December 1974 level. Then pay restraint was introduced.

The first phase was the £6 limit for settlements made between August 1975 and August 1976 (see above). During Phase I living standards recovered slightly.

As the period of the £6 limit was drawing to a close, Healey announced in his April 1976 Budget that he would reduce income tax liabilities by £1bn a year if the TUC agreed to limit wage increases to 3 per cent between August 1976 and August 1977. The TUC leadership offered a 5 per cent norm with a lower limit of £2.50 and an upper limit of £4 per week. The government agreed and the policy was ratified by a 17:1 majority at a special TUC conference in June.

Phase II should have limited average wage rises to 4½ per cent, as compared with 10 per cent under the £6 limit. In the event, average money earnings rose by about 9 per cent, implying a 6 per cent drop in real living standards over the period of the policy. This fall more than wiped out the entire recovery of the previous months.

By the end of Phase II, real earnings were at least 10 per cent lower than they had been at the close of 1974. Although data for earlier years are not strictly comparable with or as reliable as that above, they suggest that real wages had not fallen that steeply in the UK since the mid-nineteenth century.

Labour's incomes policies were not entirely to blame for the fall. Much of it had occurred in the roaring inflation before Phase I came into operation. But no Tory government could have got the TUC to accept such a fall, let alone its agreement to extend and increase it through incomes policy. Labour could and did – an important example of the valuable service that social democracy can at times perform for capital.

Callaghan had intended to introduce a Phase III with a 10 per cent ceiling. But the 1977 TUC Conference rejected further restraint, voting for immediate return to free collective bargaining. The benefits of rejection were soon apparent. Real take-home pay rose by 7 per cent between July 1977 and July 1978, the period for which Phase III had been intended.

Ever hopeful, Callaghan proposed a Phase IV with a 5 per cent ceiling for the pay round beginning August 1978. TUC Conference once again rejected restraint and workers embarked on the strike-wave which became known as the 'winter of discontent'. Some 10m working days were 'lost' between October 1978 and March 1979.

The most decisive strike was that of the Ford workers, who won 17 per cent after seven weeks out. During the strike, Labour Party conference voted against the 5 per cent policy – perhaps the most serious rebuff a Labour government had ever received from the party.

Then the lorry drivers won their first national strike for 50 years. Their very effective picketing certainly took their opponents aback. Margaret Thatcher said in the Commons at the end of January: 'Now we find that the place is practically being run by strikers' committees . . . They are "allowing" access to food. They are "allowing" certain lorries to go through . . . They have no right to prevent them from going through'.

The public sector workers fought for a £60 minimum wage. The strike showed tremendous capacity for struggle by a relatively recently organised sector, although it would perhaps have been more effective if the strength of the most strategic workers, such as those in the water industry, had been better used. Hospital workers' action in particular became a favourite target for Fleet Street hacks. One *Evening Standard* headline ran: 'Plagued by NUPE's Rats'. From the moment the dam burst on wages, Callaghan was no longer of service to capital. His government was denounced as weak and incompetent, despite his call for workers to cross picket lines.

Public spending cuts

Workers' living standards were also held down by cuts in planned social service provision. The precise extent of cuts and their effects on living standards is extremely difficult to calculate. Below is a brief account of their timing and a guess at their scale.

The February 1976 Public Expenditure White Paper expressed the intention 'broadly to stabilise the level of resources taken by government programmes after 1976–77'. Since interest on government debt was expected to grow by 20 per cent between the financial years 1976–77 and 1978–79, this implied a fall in the value of goods and services provided of about 2 per cent.

In April 1976, a system of cash limits was imposed on about three-quarters of central government expenditure (excluding social security payments), the local authority rate support grant and much local authority capital expenditure. Since the imposition of cash limits had considerably more effect on the level of public sector provision than any of the official rounds of cuts, it is worth briefly spelling out how the system works.

Before cash limits were adopted, public expenditure five-year plans were initially drawn up in constant price or volume terms (specifying a certain real level of services). Estimates of the actual current expenditures involved were then calculated by adjusting the constant price figures, first for the expected rate of inflation generally and second, for the fact that unit costs rise more rapidly on average in the public sector than in the economy as a whole because productivity rises less rapidly. The adjusted figures were often said to be enumerated in 'funny money'.

Under this system, government departments and local authorities were entitled to maintain a certain level of real provision. If the costs of providing the goods and services specified exceeded the 'funny money' estimates, the government finished up spending more than it had intended. If actual expenditure exceeded the estimate because prices rose faster than expected, then tax receipts also rose faster and additional expenditure was more or less balanced by additional revenue.

But if actual expenditure went off course because the extra growth of public sector costs exceeded the estimate, then the additional expenditure was not balanced by additional revenue. This is what had happened fairly consistently in the early seventies, as public sector pay caught up with that in the private sector, and contributed to the rapid growth of the public sector borrowing requirement during that period.

The cash limits system laid down actual cash ceilings on spending. It meant that if costs rose more rapidly than estimated, then the authorities responsible had to cut the level of real provision.

Further measures affecting expenditure in 1977–78 were announced in July 1976. This led to a demonstration of about 80,000 public sector workers in November – claimed to be the largest week-day demonstration in London since the war.

Programmes for 1977–78 and 1978–79 were pruned even more following the agreement with the IMF in December 1976 to cut £3bn off the public sector borrowing requirement over those two financial years. The 1977 expenditure White Paper envisaged further cuts in 1977–78 and zero real growth in 1978–79.

Even the cuts planned were not the end of the story, because in later years actual expenditure sank far below planned levels. Planned expenditure for 1977–78, for example, had by the start of the financial year been reduced from levels set in 1974–75 by £2.6bn. When the time came to fork out, the 1974–75 target was undercut by £5bn. Government departments systematically spent less than their official allocations. This phenomenon of 'under-spending' was carefully orchestrated by the Treasury. It was described by the head of the 1976 IMF delegation to the UK as 'a minor miracle'.

In actual fact total spending, as far as we can calculate it, was less than 4 per cent below its planned level and grew at nearly 2 per cent per year in real terms over the period of the Labour government. But the total figure is very misleading, as Table 2 shows.

2: Real Level of Government Spending: UK, 1978–79

	Indices (actual spending 1973–74 = 100)	
	Labour's plans January 1975 for 1978–79	Actual spending (after cuts)
defence	106	98
industry	63	68
(employment measures)	194	362
roads	115	93
housing	134	117
education	112	100
health	113	111
social security	123	133
debt interest	91	189
total	115	111

Source: Public Expenditure to 1978–79, *Tables 1.2, 1.3, 2.4, 3.4;* The Government's Expenditure Plans 1979–80 to 1982–83, *Tables 12 and 13.*

The deteriorating economic situation forced up certain types of spending. Debt interest doubled as the sluggishness of the economy held tax revenue more or less stagnant, and made it necessary to finance huge government deficits at increasingly high interest rates. Other programmes which grew faster than anticipated were social security, reflecting the rise in unemployment, and expenditure on various employment support schemes, which functioned largely as handouts to capital (see below). So cuts in public services were required if total government spending was not to rise much faster than intended.

The cuts destroyed any hope that the improvements in social welfare promised in the election manifesto would happen. So while the 20 per cent real increase in pensions did stop many pensioners from having to claim supplementary benefit, rising unemployment meant that the number of families living below the supplementary benefit level rose from 1976 onwards. While over a thousand comprehensive schools were formed, school building was cut by 61 per cent between 1973–74 and 1978–79. While the real cost of council house rents relative to earnings was reduced by a quarter over the period, council house building fell below the minimum level reached under the previous Tory government. While the wages of the lowest paid workers rose a little more than the average during the first two years of the Social Contract, living standards fell. So all the lowest paid gained was a smaller cut. And public spending cuts reduced by one-half the frequency with which wages inspectors checked that the paltry wages council rates were being paid. While planned health expenditure was barely cut in total, hospital building was one-third down on the 1973–74 level, threatening future deterioration in services already near collapse.

Before leaving the question of the cuts, it is perhaps worth examining why capitalists favour them. The benefit to capital of holding down wages is obvious enough. Unit costs fall; profitability and competitiveness improve. But what is in it for capital if public expenditure goes down?

In fact, high levels of public spending provide two apparent benefits for capital. First, if the government runs a large public sector borrowing requirement, this provides holders of money capital with a lucrative avenue for investment, because the state offers bonds for sale to finance the excess of expenditure over revenue. This is particularly attractive to capital at a time when the rate of profit in industry is low. In 1975, for example, interest paid on the UK national debt (i.e the cumulative total of past public sector borrowing requirements) exceeded the net profits of industrial and commercial companies.

Second, if the government runs a deficit, this assists realisation. The more government expenditure exceeds revenue, the greater total expenditure and the better the conditions for realising surplus value.

Why, then, has the CBI not only supported cuts but continually pressed for larger ones? Labour used to offer two justifications for cuts. (The Tories have since added the supposed need to finance tax-cuts to provide 'incentives'.) One of the two reasons originally given was that a large public sector borrowing requirement 'crowds out' productive investment by capital. The other was the standard, multipurpose justification for all anti-working-class policies – the need to combat inflation.

To take 'crowding out' first. It is, of course, the case that if there is full employment, the more resources are devoted to one type of activity the less there are for another. If most building workers are employed by the welfare state to build hospitals, relatively few are available to build factories for capital. The notion of 'crowding out', in the sense of the public sector depriving the private sector of real resources, makes sense *but only if there is full employment*.

Moreover, although capitalists earn interest on money lent to the government to finance welfare state expenditure, such spending seldom increases labour productivity and potential surplus value. This is true of investment as well as current expenditure. Hospital building, for example, does not necessarily reduce future NHS costs. It is done to provide better (and frequently more expensive) services. By contrast, investment in industry increases labour productivity, raises surplus value and increases competitiveness.

If public spending did 'crowd out' accumulation, it would therefore be essential from capital's point of view to try and cut it in a period of crisis.

But there was not full employment at this time. There were large numbers of people unemployed and large quantities of machinery idle. It therefore appears to make no sense whatsoever to argue that high levels of state spending would deprive the private sector of real resources. So why the pressure for cuts?

One answer lies in Labour's long-term strategy. The government intended to use wage control and other devices to hold down costs and restore profits and competitiveness. The idea was that once competitiveness improved sufficiently, exports would expand rapidly. Restored profit margins and rapid growth of foreign markets would provide conditions acceptable to capital for producing and realising surplus value. Investment would once again take off.

When this happened, high levels of public expenditure would indeed present 'crowding out' problems. As Healey said in his 1976 Budget speech, remedying the decline in UK industry would require 'a major shift in the use of our resources away from private and public consumption, towards exports and investment'. Since many of the cuts would take years to work themselves through, Labour decided to start the pruning well in advance.

But there is also a financial argument that public spending, financed by borrowing, 'crowds out' private investment, even when there is unemployment. According to this, government borrowing reduces investment by depriving firms of money capital.

The essentials of the argument are as follows. At any point in time, there is a certain volume of potential money capital (savings and credit of various kinds). The larger the government's borrowing, the larger the share of potential money capital needed by the state if it is to finance its expenditure without printing money. Interest rates have to go up too if holders of money capital are to be persuaded to lend to the state. Thus, the more the government borrows, the less credit there is around for capital, and the more expensive that credit. The effect, according to the argument, is less investment.

But there are three important objections. Firstly, there is no evidence that capital experienced a general shortage of credit under Labour (see pages 155–6). If there was any 'crowding out', it must have been because of high interest rates, rather than absolute credit shortages.

Secondly, it is highly misleading to compare interest rates of 10–15 per cent with profit rates of 3–4 per cent and to conclude that borrowing to finance productive investment was not worth while. For the interest rates quoted are *nominal* (they take no account of the fact that the loan is repaid with money whose value has been eroded by inflation), whereas the profit rates are *real*; (they do take account of inflation). Real interest rates were negative for much of the period.

Thirdly, since government spending provides markets,

heavy government borrowing has contradictory effects in increasing the incentive to invest, by improving realisation conditions, while reducing it by raising interest rates. It therefore seems unlikely that the overall effect was to dampen accumulation.

The months around the close of 1976 are perhaps an exception. The ruling class developed an irrational obsession with the size of government borrowing. If it had not been reduced then, that may indeed have led to a further collapse in investment. Capitalist paranoia can have real effects.

The other argument used to justify cuts was the claim that a large amount of government borrowing is necessarily inflationary. The crudest, monetarist, version of the argument is that a government faced with a large public sector borrowing requirement is unable to borrow enough money to cover the shortfall between tax revenues and expenditure. It is therefore compelled to print new money to finance a proportion of its spending. The result is an increase in the money supply, which means inflation.

But the argument does not depend on a specifically monetarist view about the connection between the money supply and inflation. More government borrowing means a higher level of government spending relative to tax revenue. Hence the greater will be the demand for commodities and the better the conditions for realising surplus value. The better the conditions for realisation, the likelier price rises become. So the argument about government borrowing causing inflation is not complete rubbish. But it was nevertheless very misleading of Labour to use it as a justification for cuts. This is for two reasons.

The first concerns the scale of the public sector borrowing requirement during these years. Figures of up to £10bn are often quoted. But such figures are nominal and hence misleading at a time of inflation for the same reasons as are nominal interest rates. Since the value of outstanding government debt was being eroded by inflation, much of the 'borrowing' did not add to indebtedness. It was rather a matter of the government borrowing from one source to pay back another.

In 1976, for example, the nominal public sector borrowing requirement was £8.3bn while the real figure was only £0.1bn.

National debt as a proportion of national income rose from about 45 to 48 per cent under Labour. This proportion was only about half that of the mid-60s, since when inflation had on balance eroded the value of outstanding government debt more rapidly than additional borrowing had added to it. So, although it is true that a cut in government spending counteracts inflation, it is wrong to suggest that Labour had to impose cuts because expenditure had reached levels which involved disastrous increases in national debt.

The argument is also misleading because it is incomplete. Most importantly, it lacks a class dimension. The argument is ideological because it is partial, in both senses of the term. In a sense, price rises are exactly what capital needs if profitability is low. If inflation were merely a once-off rise in prices *without repercussions* then capital would welcome it.

The worry for capital is that workers react to a higher cost of living by claiming correspondingly higher pay. Profits are prevented from rising and competitiveness is damaged by the increase in costs. This is bad enough once-off, but when, because of past inflation, people expect prices to keep going up, there is the threat of a vicious, accelerating wage/price spiral.

A cut in government borrowing works to increase unemployment because conditions for realisation deteriorate. As unemployment goes up, the working class grows weaker and finds it harder to win pay deals which keep pace with price rises. Conditions for producing surplus value improve and the likelihood of an accelerating wage/price spiral recedes.

Everyone is assumed to be against inflation, and 'anti-inflation' cuts are served up as a good thing. And so they are for capital, which benefits from deflation and less opposition from a working class weakened by unemployment. Viewed in these terms, the argument's class basis becomes obvious.

The longer-term strategic argument for cuts in state expenditure (making room for investment) and the more immediate one (fear of wage increases) are entirely consistent with each other. And they are both rational from capital's viewpoint. Cuts are essential to any strategy for resolving the crisis to capital's advantage and restoring the conditions for sustained accumulation.

Unemployment

Workers also suffered under Labour because many of them could not get jobs. The official unemployment figures show an increase from 600,000 in 1974 to just under 1½m in 1977 and 1978.

But unemployment figures are a gross underestimate of the number out of work since they count only people 'signing on' at Department of Employment offices. Many seeking work do not sign on because they are not entitled to benefit. The Cambridge Economic Policy Group has estimated the extent of unregistered unemployment during the latter period of Labour rule at about one million. Total unemployment from 1976 onwards was therefore about 2½m, or 10 per cent of the labour force. The massive waste involved in this level of unemployment is discussed in Chapter 5.

What caused mass unemployment to re-emerge? Many people believe that it happened because the rate of technological progress speeded up, so that workers were increasingly displaced by machines. This view is mistaken.

The effect of investment on jobs depends crucially on the rate at which markets grow. If markets are stagnant, so that capital is unable to sell an expanding volume of commodities, then investment in new machines will displace older, less efficient plant requiring more workers. Employment will fall overall as older machines are scrapped, and the workers operating them made redundant. Not all are re-employed on the new machines.

But if markets are expanding sufficiently fast, then old plant will be kept in operation while the new caters for the extra demand. The new machines mean more jobs; those on the old remain secure. Employment rises (though less fast than production because average labour productivity rises). So the implications of technical progress for employment depend crucially on the growth of the market.

The fundamental cause of the massive rise in unemployment under Labour was a major slowdown in the rate at which markets, and hence production, grew. The stagnation of expenditure comes across clearly in Table 3.

3: Growth of Real Expenditure: UK, 1961–78

	Average annual percentages	
	1961–73	1973–78
exports	5.6	4.0
private consumption	2.8	0.1
government expenditure	4.9	0.4
investment by capital	4.3	−1.0

Source: Cambridge Economic Policy Review, *1979, Table B3, and earlier years.*

Government spending and workers' consumption stagnated because of conscious government policies. Unemployment was not an act of God, gnomes or oil sheiks. Healey is the one to blame.

The policies were, of course, neither arbitrary nor purely vindictive. They were part of Labour's attempt to increase the rate of potential surplus value sufficiently to restore profitability and competitiveness. Labour held down government spending and workers' consumption because of the long-term decline in UK competitiveness and profitability, aggravated by the world crisis. Investment by capital tapered off because profitability was low and markets stagnant.

It may seem a little harsh to say Labour's policies caused high unemployment, given the battery of special employment schemes and training measures the government introduced. It claimed they reduced unemployment substantially. At the end of 1977, for example, 177,000 workers were said to be covered by the Temporary Employment Subsidy, 47,000 by the Job Creation Scheme and about 80,000 more by other work experience programmes and training schemes. But a number of criticisms can be levelled at the measures.

The first concerns the social usefulness of the jobs performed. Labour launched a barrage of moralistic propaganda about the importance of certain schemes in converting would-be 'vandals' into (underpaid) community workers. The Job Creation Scheme image, for example, was skilfully plagiarised from James Dean movies. It portrayed the mugger turned meals-on-wheeler.

In fact many so-called Job Creation projects smacked more of the pointless and repetitive tasks traditionally associated with military service, and performed the same primary function: disciplining potentially rebellious youth.

Moreover, the effect on employment of many of the job subsidies to capital was more apparent than real, as most of the workers would have been employed anyway. The Department of Employment reports a survey (*Gazette* July 1977) which showed that three-quarters of the young workers employed by firms claiming the school-leavers' subsidy would have been taken on regardless of the subsidy.

Other schemes attempted to avoid this happening. Applications for Temporary Employment Subsidy, for example –a scheme which paid £20 per week for a year for each worker kept on who would otherwise have been made redundant – were supposedly carefully scrutinised.

If such schemes really did save jobs, they would be enormously attractive to government, since the costs involved would be far lower than the ensuing financial gains. The government would save on dole money and collect tax from a worker who would otherwise have been sacked. That's the theory. And the Department of Employment calculated that in the case of the Temporary Employment Scheme, 'flowback to the Exchequer might amount to three-quarters of the workers' earnings', so that, if the job paid £60 a week, the government not only saved a job, but also made itself £45 for an expenditure of £20. Pure magic!

In fact, the exercise was more like an inept conjuring trick, because a job saved in one company usually meant a similar one lost elsewhere. With a given level of demand for commodities, higher output and employment in one subsidised company necessarily means lower output and employment in a non-subsidised competitor. Total employment is increased only to the extent that subsidies increase total expenditure, and hence demand for commodities, or lead to the use of more labour-intensive production techniques. There is little reason to believe either of these happened to a substantial extent.

So a Temporary Employment Scheme subsidy usually meant the Exchequer paid out £20 to one company, and a job got lost in another. Suppose the second company then claimed its subsidy.

The total cost to the exchequer went up to £40, and a job got lost in a third company. And so on.

It is unlikely that the whole paraphernalia of employment schemes had any real effect on the overall level of unemployment. The government, holding back the growth of markets by cuts in government spending and real wages, was merely nominating who was to be on the dole.

The continued decline of British capital

Despite Labour's success in holding down wages and the whole battery of tax allowances and subsidies introduced for capital, the rate of profit had risen only slightly above the catastrophically low levels of 1974–75 by the time the Callaghan government left office (Table 4).

4: Rates of Profit for UK Industrial and Commercial Companies, 1973–78

	before tax %	after tax %
1973	7.2	5.7
1974	3.9	3.3
1975	3.5	2.2
1976	3.8	2.3
1977	4.5	2.5
1978	4.7	2.9

Bank of England Quarterly Bulletin, *June 1979, p. 183.*

Further, the rapid growth of profit from North Sea oil accounts for a significant proportion of the increase. These profits were insignificant in 1974–75 but had risen to about 15 per cent of the total by the end of 1978. North Sea oil profits should be considered separately from those appropriated by other industrial and commercial companies, since they go to the international oil companies who have no reason to re-invest them in the UK.

In fact North Sea oil, paradoxically, reduced profits in

industry. The availability of oil benefited the balance of payments by virtually eliminating the need for fuel imports, which in 1974 accounted for about one-seventh of total imports. This improvement brought a sharp appreciation of sterling during the latter months of 1978 and the spring and summer of 1979.

The balance of payments usually improves because domestic capital is better able to compete with foreign rivals. Imports are reduced and/or exports increased. The currency then appreciates and reduces competitiveness by raising prices relative to those charged by foreign rivals. Appreciation is usually due to better competitiveness, and then partially offsets its effects.

The gain to the balance of payments due to North Sea oil had nothing to do with improved competitiveness. It was the result of a limited natural resource becoming available. The balance of payments looked better because of this buried treasure, which could be sold for dollars over the course of a decade or so, not because industrial productivity had improved at all.

Sterling appreciated anyway, and this weakened competitiveness in the normal way. But there was no underlying improvement. Sterling's appreciation aggravated a situation that was already deteriorating, rather than dampening down gains from a positive one.

UK capital could ill afford more deterioration in competitiveness, which had continued to weaken under Labour. The UK's share of world manufacturing exports temporarily stopped shrinking. It was 9.4 per cent in 1973 and 9.5 per cent in 1978. But this was achieved only at the expense of a more rapid rise in the foreign currency price of UK exports relative to those of major competitors. The volume of UK manufactured exports rose by only 21 per cent between 1973 and 1978, while that of world manufacturing exports rose by 30 per cent. This development was clearly not sustainable. The UK also continued to import increasingly more goods. By the middle of 1979 imports of finished manufactures were 70 per cent higher than in 1973, while total manufacturing production in the UK stayed unchanged.

Things continued to deteriorate because British capital increased labour productivity less than one third as fast as its major rivals. Output per person hour in manufacturing rose by only 5 per cent in the UK between 1973 and 1978. Over the same period it rose by 15 per cent in the US, 17 per cent in Italy, 20 per cent in W. Germany, 21 per cent in France and 22 per cent in Japan.

Two factors account for the gap between UK and foreign productivity levels growing even wider. Firstly, accumulation was still stagnant. Manufacturing investment was no higher in 1978 than in 1974, leaving the growth rate of the manufacturing capital stock at less than 2 per cent, well below the rate for major competitors. Because the rate of profit was low and markets stagnant, capitalists stayed reluctant to invest. The contradictory effects of attempting to improve the conditions for the production of surplus value by wage restraint and deflationary cuts in public spending plans are plain. Markets stagnated; and the improvement in profitability, such as it was, did not feed through into more investment.

Secondly, stagnation of markets meant that UK capacity was even more underused than its competitors and this meant low productivity. Healey's hope that an export boom would provide the markets to justify increased investment foundered on stagnation in the world economy and on British capital's inability to cut into foreign markets without achieving a big increase in productivity.

Given sluggish investment, the only way of pushing up productivity would have been through massive industrial rationalisation. This would have involved concentrating production on the most efficient plants, driving up productivity through speedup, elimination of traditional work practices and so forth.

Employment in manufacturing industry was cut by 7 per cent between 1974 and 1978. But this was hardly greater than the fall in production, so productivity edged up only slightly. This suggests a pattern of defensive rationalisation. As sales stagnated, some old plants were closed down. Industries like electrical engineering, where cuts in employment were achieved as production was expanded, were exceptional. Aggressive rationalisation of this kind, yielding higher sales by driving up productivity and competing more effectively on world markets, was much more extensive in Europe and Japan.

The extent to which this failure was bound up with Labour

government policies is difficult to determine. On the one hand, the 'industrial strategy' was intended to increase productivity and Labour encouraged rationalisation in National Enterprise Board companies, especially British Leyland. On the other hand, job subsidies, which propped up less efficient firms for a time, showed the government's ambivalence. It wanted rationalisation, but not the implied rise in unemployment. Nor was it prepared to encourage more thoroughgoing rationalisation by creating even higher unemployment.

A government affects the prevailing situation both economically, in terms of general policies and politically, in terms of how actively it encourages capital to force through rationalisation against labour movement opposition. The Labour government, despite its humiliating retreats, still responded to labour movement pressure to an extent excessive from capital's point of view.

Balance sheet and legacy

The Labour government fulfilled some valuable functions for capital. Most importantly, it dampened the mass radicalisation which had developed under Heath and used the social contract to pull the economy back from a wage/price spiral which had threatened to accelerate into hyperinflation.

But the benefits to capital were temporary and limited. The Labour leadership became less willing to implement extensive public spending cuts as its period in office drew to a close, fearing uncontainable opposition from both party and unions. Its initial success on the wages front also proved short-lived. Votes at TUC conferences and the strike wave of 1978–79 showed clearly that Callaghan had lost support for voluntary wages restraint. The government's unwillingness to push up unemployment further, and its reluctance to accept the logic of driving up productivity regardless of the effect on jobs, stood in the way of the all-out rationalisation drive needed to improve competitiveness.

The most important lesson of the 1974–79 Labour government is that Callaghan-type policies are inadequate to the needs of UK capital. The measures he employed proved incapable of stemming economic decline, let alone reversing it. Both the ruling class and the labour movement have begun to look elsewhere for radical policies to restore conditions for sustained economic growth. Labour's failures thus paved the way for Thatcher's policies, which could never have been implemented in the context of the relation of class forces existing in 1974.

5.
Into the Eighties

The world context

Unless the labour movement suffers major defeats, of which there are no signs at present, it is unlikely that capital will recreate conditions for rapid accumulation in the next few years. But will the situation in the world economy deteriorate sharply?

It is improbable that governments would willingly engineer a slump on the scale of the thirties, when output in the capitalist world fell by 19 per cent. Those in the weakest economies may try severe deflationary policies. Thatcher already has. But those in major economies – the US (accounting for 38 per cent of world-capitalist output), Japan (13 per cent) and W. Germany (10 per cent) – do not face such immediately pressing problems. Savage deflation would not be in their interest. The economic and political risks of engineering it would be too great. But could their economies crash anyway?

Only if investment fell sharply. Workers' expenditure is not capricious enough to provoke a crash. Stagnation alone will not bring one about, either. Slow market growth and the development of cheaper production techniques make it worth while for capital to accumulate slowly. So what could spark off a collapse of investment?

If governments suddenly went in for protectionism in a big way, this could in principle disrupt markets sufficiently to spark off a crash. But governments are aware of this, and, unless there is some other major shock to the system, are likely to accompany protectionist measures with bilateral trade arrangements. If investment dropped as trade fell, they would probably take mildly reflationary measures.

A major financial crisis seems more likely to provoke a

crash. If credit were tightened abruptly, this could precipitate a chain of major bankruptcies, panic sales of stocks to retain solvency, a slashing of investment programmes and a collapse in demand for goods sold on credit. The combination could result in spiralling slump. But what could precipitate such a crisis?

Developments within a national economy would be unlikely to do so without massive and deliberate deflation. Even where credit is stretched as severely as in the US, borrowers' difficulties can be overcome by giving them more time to repay and the state can bail out banks in difficulties.

Some third world countries might refuse to pay up and opt out of the capitalist financial system altogether. But even if they did, international banking consortia would share the losses, and central banks would step in to prevent major bank failures.

The biggest threat to financial stability is undoubtedly the vulnerability of the dollar. Only a small proportion of dollar holdings need move into other currencies to force the US government into putting up interest rates steeply and restricting credit to prevent further speculation. But who would move out of the dollar in a big way?

Very few powerful groups would benefit economically from the collapse of the dollar. Governments of other major capitalist economies fear the damage a slump in the US would inflict on the world economy. And a flight from the dollar would leave them unable to control their money supplies. Other major dollar holders, who are seldom in a position to transfer all their assets into other currencies at a stroke, fear the capital losses they would sustain if the dollar began to tumble.

This does not mean there will not be bouts of speculation against the dollar. But it does suggest that many private dollar holders will think hard before taking part, and that central banks will continue to intervene to support the dollar.

It is conceivable that developments in the Middle East might prompt OPEC countries to withdraw dollar holdings to put pressure on the US. This would be extremely costly to the oil producers since they would not be able to withdraw all funds simultaneously and might suffer enormous losses if the dollar began to crash. It would also be extremely risky. The US might respond by seizing and freezing all OPEC monies in US banks, for example. However, political considerations could over-ride the economic arguments against the move.

So if a major crash occurring for narrowly economic reasons seems unlikely, a politically motivated assault on the dollar could trigger one off. The over-extended international credit system and the vulnerability of the world's major currency make it possible.

The US government knows it, and so refrains from expansionary policies which could add to pressure on the dollar. It has no way of gauging how far it could safely expand. So even if slump is avoided, the fragility of the credit system will remain an important influence maintaining stagnation in the world economy.

A major slump would have such unpredictable effects that it is fruitless to speculate on the sequence of events that would follow. We have little choice but to analyse the possibilities for regenerating the UK economy against the more probable backcloth of continued stagnation in the world economy. We look at three contending strategies.

The only important features they share are recognition that past policies have failed to restore British capitalism to health and belief that more drastic treatment is required. Since few would disagree, all three approaches stand reasonable chances of winning support. Class struggle over economic policy in the eighties will, we believe, focus increasingly on these three contending approaches.

The two which have already won large-scale support, Thatcherism and the Alternative Economic Strategy (AES), also share another important feature. They are based on the conviction that it is possible to regenerate the economy on a capitalist basis. They aim to restore the conditions for full employment, rising living standards and sustained growth while leaving the ownership and control of the bulk of industry largely in private hands.

This belief is about all that Thatcherism and the strategy have in common. They differ crucially on whether the economy can be regenerated without damaging workers' interests and on the nature of the policies required. This difference reflects diametrically opposed class interests.

The third approach, that of a planned socialist economy, like the Alternative Economic Strategy, is based on the conviction that the UK economy can and should be regenerated by implementing policies to protect workers' immediate economic interests. But, in contrast to the AES, it holds that this aim can be achieved only by depriving capital of the ownership and control of industry.

Thatcherism

Many workers believe that the policies of the new Tory right are irrational, in that they do not reflect the real interests of capital (or, indeed, of any other class or social group). They see Thatcherism as an outmoded nineteenth century ideology with little relevance to contemporary economic reality. This view is understandable, given the absurd way in which many of the policies are presented. It is, however, wrong.

The core of Thatcherism is a coherent set of policies aimed at enabling market forces to restore adequate conditions for producing surplus value. All other considerations are subordinated to this aim.

The main policies intended to bring about this improvement are:

- Tight monetary policy
- Cuts in public spending
- Cuts in (especially direct) taxation
- Cuts in state aid to industry
- Legal restraints on trade union activity.

It is worth briefly considering each.

Monetarism

Tight monetary policy, or 'monetarism', is perhaps the best-known and least understood of Tory policies. It has in recent years acquired considerable mystique.

Contrary to the idea that monetarism is simply about controlling inflation, the essence of Tory monetarism is the belief that tight control of the money supply is an extremely powerful device for restoring competitiveness to industry. The Tory cabinet considers this justified according it priority over all other economic objectives.

Basically, the idea is to hold down the money supply's

growth rate. Credit becomes progressively harder to get, and more expensive. The result is less expenditure and more bankruptcies. Fewer goods are bought on credit and as sales fall, companies find they are less able to cover cash deficits by borrowing. The policy is thus deflationary, and increases unemployment.

Monetarism improves the conditions for producing surplus value in a number of ways. By driving the least efficient companies in an industry out of business it raises average labour productivity within each sector. By driving proportionately more firms in the least internationally competitive industries out of existence, it concentrates production in sectors with relatively favourable conditions for producing surplus value. Monetarism therefore improves average production conditions by shifting the balance of companies and industries in favour of the more productive.

The destruction of weak companies also releases resources for use in strong ones. Machinery previously owned by an inefficient company may, after bankruptcy, be bought up and used more productively by an efficient one. After bankruptcy, workers with a history of strong plant level organisation may find they can only get jobs in companies without such organisation. They may find themselves forced to work more intensively. Bankruptcies thus facilitate the transfer of resources from low to high productivity employment.

A tight monetary policy also tends to improve productivity in relatively efficient companies. By making credit difficult, markets tight and failure more likely, it puts pressure on management to improve the way production is organised. Capital puts up with inefficient practices when the economic climate is healthy and profits assured, but stamps on them when bankruptcy threatens.

By increasing unemployment, monetarism dampens workers' willingness and ability to resist heavier work loads. People are understandably reluctant to take a tough stand on job conditions if bankruptcy seems possible and the chances of finding another job are low.

It is not just a matter of individual demoralisation, important though that is. Workers' collective organisations are weakened by high levels of unemployment. The financial strength of trade unions, and hence their ability to protect job conditions, is damaged by high unemployment among their membership.

Unemployment also breeds illegal work conditions. Many workers will accept jobs in which they forfeit all legal and trade union protection if the only alternative is a lengthy spell on the dole. Employers who do not have to worry about safety or strikes can often devise fiendishly effective schemes for increasing productivity.

Finally, tight control of the money supply also holds down money wages. The mechanisms are essentially the same as those affecting productivity. Managements resist wage claims because of the threat of bankruptcy, workers fear losing their jobs, trade unions regard lengthy strikes as too costly, workers accept illegal jobs at appallingly low rates of pay, and so on.

Lower money wage increases mean higher profits, and to some extent lower inflation, as the pressure of the stagnant market forces companies to pass on some of the effect of smaller wage increases.

Thatcher's stress on the money supply is somewhat misleading. The core of the policy is really deflation and more unemployment. This can be achieved either by cutting the money supply and putting up interest rates (monetary measures), or by cutting public spending and tinkering with taxation (fiscal measures). In fact, almost all deflationary packages involve both. The specific role of tight credit is to ensure that weak firms cannot hang on by getting deeper and deeper into debt.

Cuts in tax and public spending

The general role public spending cuts play in improving conditions for producing surplus value has already been discussed (in Chapter 4 above). The main way in which Tory cuts differ from Labour's is that they are aimed particularly at cutting state employment.

Cuts in state employment clearly complement the Tories' deflationary policy of pushing up unemployment. Some of them also fall in with capital's more immediate interests. It is, for example, desirable for the hard-pressed construction industry to have cuts in housing expenditure fall on direct labour departments rather than on contracts with the private sector.

Tax cuts played a major role in the Tories' election campaign and are an important plank of their programme. They are usually justified as 'essential to give new incentives to effort, enterprise and efficiency' (CBI). Quite why tax cuts should foster these classic capitalist virtues is unclear. The return of a few pop stars from tax exile is unlikely to cure the UK's economic ills.

It is tempting to see disproportionate cuts for high income earners simply as handouts to the Tories' most loyal supporters. But they do play a role in the overall strategy. Reducing tax on high incomes, including those composed of dividends and interest payments, increases the surplus value available to capital and its agents for accumulation.

Cuts in the standard rate of income tax are intended 'to help secure wage moderation' (CBI). The idea is that workers are concerned only with take-home pay whereas capital has to cough up gross pre-tax wages. If income tax is reduced, then take-home pay can go up while gross pay stays the same, so capital's wage costs are held down.

The problem is that tax cuts which expand purchasing power offset the desired deflationary effect of reductions in public spending and undermine other components of the strategy. So while deflation is the main objective tax cuts have to take second place.

Aid to industry

Cutting industrial aid can improve the conditions for producing surplus value as follows. Companies in which productivity is so low that the value of output is less than that of the wage would go out of business without subsidies. Their extinction would raise average productivity.

Secondly, subsidies may encourage companies to adopt low productivity techniques by making input artificially cheap. Employment support schemes have this effect on wages. Do away with subsidies, and average productivity goes up.

Finally, ending subsidies removes some protection against losses and bankruptcy. Deflationary policies improve potential surplus value all the more effectively when not impeded by attempts to prop up precisely those firms that have to be forced out.

The policy of 'clear financial discipline' for nationalised industries, combined with what the CBI describes as 'commercial pricing', fits in with the general approach of not protecting low efficiency producers.

Anti-trade union legislation

The final policy to consider is legal restriction of trade union activity. *Labour Research* has summed up the Tories' proposals as:

> Drastic limitation of the right to picket, severe reduction of the right to call sympathetic and blacking strikes against suppliers and customers, a renewed attack on the closed shop, blatant interference on the right of unions to run their affairs in accordance with their own rules and interference by a government official in the administration of union ballots. (September 1979, p. 196)

The object is to weaken unions, especially at shop-floor level. This would facilitate market forces holding down wages and increasing rationalisation, and hence help to increase potential surplus value.

So Thatcherism is a coherent package to improve conditions for producing surplus value. But the strategy would lack coherence if it had no solution to realisation difficulties.

The problem of realisation

Much Tory writing suggests that realisation is unproblematic. Sir Keith Joseph, for example, sketches the following picture of the recuperative powers of the market:

> The labour and resources shed by some industries are re-allocated to expanding industries, to infant businesses and to new economic growth – provided they are not obstructed . . . Full employment – or nearly full – and rising living standards will provide themselves if we let them. (*Towards Fuller Employment*, p. 22)

He seems to believe that if problems in surplus value production are solved, then realisation will take care of itself. But realisation problems will not disappear just because leading Tories fail to acknowledge them.

There are two ways in which such problems could in principle be resolved within the context of the strategy. One would be for the UK to win a bigger share of world markets, as described above (in Chapter 1). If potential surplus value were improved sufficiently to make UK capital internationally competitive, it could begin to expand at the expense of foreign rivals.

The second possibility is reflation. If rationalisation were carried through successfully, leading to a spectacular improvement in the conditions for producing surplus value, conditions which the government were confident could be maintained in an expansion, then pump-priming would stimulate accumulation. The regular introduction of new techniques would then generate sustained productivity growth which would prevent increases in real wages eroding potential surplus value.

So Thatcherism could in principle solve problems in both the production and realisation of surplus value, thereby recreating the conditions for sustained accumulation. In that sense, it is a coherent and viable strategy for the ruling class. That is the theory. It will almost certainly fare otherwise in practice.

Can the strategy succeed?

The first problem the policy may face concerns the scale of unemployment and bankruptcy required. The strategy requires firms and jobs pruned to the point at which the reduced 'core' of economic activity is conducted on the basis of conditions for producing surplus value regarded as adequate by capital and internationally competitive. Only after this point has been reached can sustained and profitable accumulation take place and employment expand. But how long a dole queue does this mean? How many bankruptcies will there be? How big a 'core' would be left?

It could be miniscule. It may be necessary for unemployment to grow, and economic activity to decline beyond a point that is even temporarily economically sustainable. Some production is essential to maintain the population, even if most of it is on the dole. The viable 'core' might be smaller than this indispensable minimum.

It is not that the authorities have neglected to calculate the size of the 'core', since it is impossible to know in advance how far the process has to go. The scale of unemployment required to break worker resistance to a marked deterioration in job conditions – to take just one example of the factors involved – cannot, by its nature, be reliably estimated in advance. The proof of the monetarist pudding is, after all, in the eating.

To sum up, even if all goes smoothly and under the firm control of the authorities, there is no guarantee that the result will be economically viable. And what if it gets out of control?

Monetarist policies improve conditions for producing surplus value, and hence long-term profitability, only by means of processes which depress profits in the short run. The tighter realisation conditions which lie at the heart of the strategy make it difficult to pass cost increases on in full. By restricting markets tight realisation conditions also increase unit costs by reducing the volume of output over which fixed costs are spread. An increase in wages, and other direct costs relative to prices is, of course, essential to initiate enough scrapping to drive low efficiency producers out of business. But the profits of high efficiency producers also come under pressure.

The only way to avoid weakening even the strongest units of capital temporarily would be to hold down wages and increase productivity substantially and rapidly in stronger companies, while driving weaker ones out of business quickly. The strength of the working class means that capital finds it difficult to push up productivity rapidly. So even the staunchest advocates of Thatcherism would probably agree that things have to get worse before they can get better.

But suppose capitalist confidence collapsed. If capital were to panic at some point in the process and stopped investing altogether there could be a slide into slump. And the authorities might lose all control over the process.

The state's demand-management policies control realisation conditions, and hence the level of economic activity, only within limits. If capitalists' expectations about the shape of things to come strays beyond the spectrum of controlled pessimism to guarded optimism, pump-priming techniques will not work. Suppose, for instance, capitalists thought summary expropriation was likely. No amount of pump priming would generate an investment boom.

More narrowly economic developments can also give rise to expectations which render demand-management policies ineffective. The possibility of reflation giving rise to speculation and accelerating inflation, without significantly increasing accumulation, has already been discussed. It very nearly happened in the seventies.

It is equally possible for capitalist pessimism to reach a level at which pump priming fails to prevent a collapse of production (and, perhaps, prices). The single-minded pursuit of monetarism could spark off a collapse of confidence which would generate slump on a scale to rival that of the 1930s.

Capitalist confidence is shaped by a wide variety of factors and is highly volatile. It is therefore perfectly possible for the authorities to guess wrongly about capital's response to developments which otherwise pan out precisely as expected. And, of course, things may take an unexpected turn.

External markets are one important dimension of potential instability. The authorities have to make assumptions about the rate at which foreign markets will grow to estimate the scale of deflation that particular policies will achieve. It is possible that governments in a number of countries might simultaneously attempt controlled deflation of their economies on the incorrect assumption that others were not doing likewise, and hence that foreign markets would not contract. The result would be a far greater fall in output than any had expected, with the accompanying danger of capitalist confidence collapsing.

These, then, are the narrowly economic reasons why Thatcherism might fail even if pursued consistently. But political factors place severe obstacles in the way of its systematic implementation. The following assessment of them looks at how capital and labour are likely to respond to the strategy.

Capital's response

Capital's response to Thatcherism has been cautious so far. It recognises that previous policies failed to reverse the process of decline and acknowledges the need for a more radical approach. It is also aware that the crux of the problem is the need for extensive rationalisation.

But the CBI, *The Economist* and the *Financial Times* have all regularly warned Thatcher not to go too far too fast. When the Tories were elected the CBI argued against a budget

> designed to depress the level of activity. Profits remain very low: unemployment is likely to start to rise; and – of course with some important exceptions – lack of demand remains the most important factor limiting output by industry and commerce . . . no monetary target should even be so rigid or restrictive that trade and industry are unable over considerable periods to obtain credit for profitable expansion or reasonable terms (*Economic Policy and Budget Representations* . . ., pp. 9 and 24)

In other words, go easy.

The CBI has called for state intervention in industry to be limited and subsidies cut, but added that 'state aid schemes are justified if they seek to assist industries facing unfair foreign competition, or strategically vital industries (defence) or to ensure the transfer of resources into a viable sector (transectional aid)' and would even support the bailing out of major firms whose financial difficulties could lead to 'serious disruption to other companies or industries' (*The Road to Recovery*, p. 51).

Capital is less than wholehearted in its support for Thatcherism because it realises that, while drastic remedies may be necessary, they will hurt, at least in the short term. It is one thing to accept in principle that the weak should go to the wall. It is altogether a different matter to accept that one's own company is failing and should not be bailed out.

Weak companies are not the only ones that feel faint-hearted about Thatcherism. The strong, also liable to be squeezed badly, may consider the strategy broadly correct, but would rather not set a date for its full-blooded implementation.

It is in our view quite likely that capital will continually urge moderation; and even argue for reversal of the plan at times. If Thatcher's strategy does not seem to be working well and quickly, and profits get squeezed, capital may push for controlled expansion to improve profitability temporarily. Heath-style policies could regain Tory support. The likely outcome would be a brief period of expansion, followed by a further stagnation. This would not be immediately catastrophic for capital, but it would not offer any prospect of long-term improvement either.

The workers' response

Effective opposition to Tory policies is, however, more likely to come from the working class than from disgruntled capitalists. Mass trade union action against Thatcherism seems a likely first step. The Tories are well aware of this possibility and of its implications.

An unofficial Conservative Party report by Nicholas Ridley combines unrealistic trickery – arguing that the government 'take on' only weak unions, where necessary rigging profits figures in 'vulnerable sectors' of the nationalised industries (i.e. ones in which the unions are strong) to justify giving in to claims – with confrontationist bluster: 'There should be a large and mobile squad of police equipped and prepared to uphold the law against violent picketing. Good non-union drivers should be recruited to cross picket-lines with police protection.'

A leaked report by Lord Carrington to the Tory leadership is more realistic:

> Strong unions and advanced technology operated by their members, particularly in fuel and power, mean that no government these days can 'win' in the way Mr Baldwin's Cabinet triumphed during the General Strike of 1926 by maintaining supplies and services.
> The group examined the possibility of using the Armed Forces to break strikes and concluded that such a practice could not be adopted on a large scale for two reasons: first that Britain no longer had enough troops and second that it would permanently damage the fabric and practice of the country's politics. (*The Times*, 18 April 1978)

Thatcher must sleep uneasy at the prospect of an exit like Heath's.

The AES – a way forward for the Labour movement?

If, as seems highly possible, Thatcher's plans were scotched by the trade union movement, what then? The labour movement would not be satisfied with a re-run of 1974–79 Labour government policies.

By the end of Labour's career in office, the right-wing leadership was coming under serious pressure from its rank and file. The increasingly hostile membership was weary of years of anti-working-class policies and a lack of future perspective. Some of the more prominent Labour figures chose to desert to the greener pastures of the European Commission, TV and so on.

The leadership of the left of the party initially had little to do with the increasing pressure on the right wing. It had failed to campaign openly for a clear alternative to pro-capitalist policies during the life of the government (Chapter 4), and before the election it feebly accepted a manifesto well to the right of Labour's previous one, because Callaghan threatened to resign otherwise.

Without any real lead from the left of the parliamentary party many activists focused their frustration on the issue of democracy within the party. This process was exemplified by the epic struggle of constituency members in Newham North East to replace their sitting MP, Reg Prentice, who had distinguished himself by the bluntness of his anti-working-class statements.

The campaign for Labour Party democratisation has since gathered momentum and been adopted by Benn and many leading Tribunites. The 1979 conference decided that constituencies would automatically reselect their MPs between each General Election and that the manifesto would be written by the national executive. The right wing's grip on the party is being seriously eroded.

This is important. It means the ruling class cannot count on the value of collaboration with right-wing Labour Party leaders, who might be willing enough to support anti-working-class measures, but would risk being renounced by their party.

If the left won full control of the Labour Party, this would also mean that parliamentary party policy would be brought into line with that of the party as a whole, in which case it would almost certainly take up the Alternative Economic Strategy seriously.

The last Labour government ditched the 1972–74 Alternative Economic Strategy, a move which discredited the parliamentary party leadership in the eyes of many militants and political activists. But it did not discredit the strategy, which remains the dominant alternative to pro-capitalist policies.

One variant or another is the official policy of the Labour Party as a whole (Labour's *Programme For Britain 1976* passed by Conference), of the TUC and of the Communist Party. There is considerable rank and file support for it throughout the labour movement, almost certain to grow as Tory policies bite deeper.

Nor is support for such policies confined to the UK. Large sections of the European labour movement have in recent years adopted an approach similar to that of the Tribunites and the British Communist Party.

Below we assess the AES in a manner consistent with our analysis of the extent and nature of the crisis. Many advocates of

1: Alternative Economic Strategy

	Problems	Policies
I	production and employment	a. expand the economy, tax cuts and public spending increases
		b. 35 hour week
II	inflation	price controls
III	investment	a. selective nationalisation—NEB to take over 20–25 profitable manufacturing firms
		b. nationalisation of banks
		c. planning agreements
IV	balance of payments	import controls
V	distribution of wealth	wealth tax
VI	relations in the factory	'industrial democracy'—workers on supervisory boards

the AES view recent economic developments differently, and in our view incorrectly. (For example, Stuart Holland, chief architect of the original 1972–74 programme, consistently underestimates the extent to which profitability has declined).

We assess the strategy as a programme for the labour movement. We treat the policies as component parts of an overall strategy rather than as a mixed bag of proposals, and ask whether the strategy is capable of achieving economic recovery *while protecting workers' immediate interests*.

Since there is no formally authorised version of the strategy we have drawn up the composite summary shown in Table 1 on p. 149. We doubt that supporters of the AES will think it unfair.

Our criticisms of the strategy, which we do not believe is viable, are offered in a constructive spirit as a contribution to discussion within the workers' movement.

Expand the economy

All proponents of the AES argue for an expansion of the economy as a first step towards eliminating unemployment. The Communist Party, for example, writes:

> There is only one way to expand the economy and that is by an incentive to increase output. The only incentive . . . is to ensure a market for increased output. The only way to ensure a market for the increased output is to increase the demand which is within Britain's control . . . That in turn means an end to wages and public spending cuts. (Ramelson, p. 22)

Some of the weaker, 'Keynesian' variants of the strategy appear to suggest that only the balance of payments would face serious problems as a result of such expansion. These, they argue, could be remedied with import controls (on which, see below).

This view is in many ways the other side of the coin to the crudest version of Thatcherism, which sees the conditions for producing surplus value as the only problem, and ignores realisation conditions. Vulgar keynesian variants of the strategy concern themselves solely with realisation and ignore problems in the production of surplus value.

Expansion based on higher living standards for workers

would rapidly run into difficulties. Higher pay means lower potential surplus value. Profitability might initially be maintained, or even rise a little, as capacity utilisation rose and actual surplus value approached potential. But this development would prove short-lived. Capital would not undertake the substantial productive investment required to raise productivity and maintain the impetus of the boom because potential surplus value would be inadequate.

As full employment was approached, and the newly-strengthened working class pressed for further wage increases, prices would have to rise faster to maintain the already inadequate rate of potential surplus value. This would provoke a wage/price spiral, damaging competitiveness, threatening hyperinflation and diverting investment into speculative avenues. The result would be similar to the ill-fated Barber boom of 1972–73.

An economic strategy for the working class should certainly include demands to keep up wages, reverse cuts and start more public works. But such measures alone would not cure the system's ailments. On the contrary, they would create further difficulties. Such gains could be consolidated only in the context of a programme capable of dealing with the problems they would give rise to.

Price controls

The Communist Party and others propose a thorough system of price controls to suppress inflation after an expansion of expenditure. If the measures were sufficiently thorough, they could by definition prevent prices accelerating. But the effects on profitability would be disastrous. Potential surplus value would be squeezed still further by real wage increases, scrapping would accelerate, bankruptcies would proliferate and the initial rise in employment would rapidly be reversed.

The 35-hour week

Many AES supporters also propose the immediate implementation of a 35-hour week as a solution to unemployment. In 1977 full-time employees in the UK worked 41.3 hours per week on average. If these were cut to 37 (by reducing the 'normal' working week to 35 hours and average overtime from three to two hours, for example) then 10 per cent more jobs would in principle be created 'at a stroke' and unemployment eliminated.

But would less hours mean less pay? Many strategy advocates are evasive about this. John Hughes, for example, in a detailed discussion of many aspects of the demand, lamely notes that a part of the extra cost to capital 'is likely to be offset . . . by the greater willingness of organised labour – in return for the shorter working week – to settle for more moderate advances in weekly pay' (Hughes, p. 114). But this avoids the issue. Keeping real wages pegged, let alone 'moderate' increases, would be absolutely disastrous for capital. And 'moderate' increases in money wages at a time of high inflation imply cuts in real earnings.

A 35-hour week with no loss of pay would raise costs by about 10 per cent. If this increase could not be passed on in higher prices, conditions for producing surplus value would suffer badly. Profits would fall by some 50 per cent. Scrapping and bankruptcies would accelerate and unemployment would soar far above present levels.

If, on the other hand, pay were cut in proportion to hours, living standards would fall by about 10 per cent. Most workers would find this quite unacceptable.

Capital would also oppose the move because, although it would leave unit costs more or less unchanged, it would strengthen the working class, by temporarily providing full employment, and make it more determined to secure wage increases to offset the fall in living standards. Future improvements in the conditions for producing surplus value would become harder to achieve.

Finally, if the working week were shortened without a cut in money wages, and capital were able to pass on the cost increase in higher prices, then either real wages would eventually fall by the required 10 per cent or so or a severe wage/price spiral would set in.

None of these difficulties would be resolved by the simultaneous introduction of the 35-hour week in all advanced-capitalist countries. It is, of course, true that a co-ordinated move would avoid problems of relative competitiveness. But a deterioration in competitiveness is by no means the only objection from

capital's point of view. All the difficulties discussed above apply
as much on an international as on a national scale.

The international labour movement's campaign for a 35-
hour week with no loss of pay is an important one. But in itself, it
offers no solution. Brought in without other policies to protect
workers from its contradictory effects, a 35-hour week would
create enormous problems.

Some of the measures discussed above would leave the
problems of producing surplus value unaffected. Others would
exacerbate them. None would solve them. This is their fundamental weakness.

Capital will not voluntarily embark on sustained accumulation if conditions for producing surplus value are not favourable.
So the strategy must include measures to deal with the problem of
potential surplus value, either by improving the conditions for
producing surplus value, or by persuading capital to invest despite
poor profitability.

Incomes policy

An incomes policy might improve conditions for producing
surplus value. Many AES supporters, including the Communist
Party, are opposed to the idea. But others advocate the notion of a
'socialist' incomes policy. Indeed, the leading Tribunite, Brian
Sedgemore, goes so far as to say that the strategy would not work
without one.

But an incomes policy could solve the problem only by
cutting real wages severely. If this is what Sedgemore is advocat-
ing, then it is no more socialist than Callaghan's policies, and has
about as much chance of winning favour with the labour movement. It certainly would not defend workers' immediate interests.

But there is room for doubt as to what Sedgemore has in
mind: 'what has been wrong with incomes policies to date is that
they have all been used in periods of economic depression to shift
resources from wages to profits' (Sedgemore, p. 40). An incomes
policy which did not achieve such a shift would do nothing to
improve conditions for producing surplus value and would be
pointless if the idea were to coax investment along.

Selective nationalisations

Selective nationalisations, along the lines of Labour's 1972–74 programme (see Chapter 4), is one influential proposal designed to persuade capital to invest in unfavourable conditions. The theory is developed most fully by its principal architect, Stuart Holland, in his book *The Socialist Challenge*.

According to Holland, the 25 or so newly nationalised companies would not only carry out expanded investment programmes of their own (*Tribune* has often mentioned the figure of £1000m per year) but also exert a 'pull effect on other big firms,' based on

> oligopoly leadership, or the situation in which one of the new firms at the top end of an industry breaks from the pack and pioneers a new product or technique on a major scale. While the remaining leading firms might otherwise have hung around and delayed introducing a similar project or process, they cannot any longer afford to do so without risk of losing sales, profits and market share to the pioneer firm. (Holland, p. 185)

This argument is totally unconvincing.

The lack of a fiercely competitive environment may have been a problem in the forties and fifties (see Chapter 2). But now British capital suffers from too much competition, rather than too little. It cannot stand up to its rivals abroad. Inadequate conditions for producing and realising surplus value are the fundamental problems today, and Holland gives no convincing reasons why private capital would emulate 'exemplary' behaviour by newly nationalised companies in such conditions. If companies think ventures will be sufficiently profitable, then they will undertake them. If not, as is by and large the case at present, they will not.

Ironically, the CBI has objected to selective nationalisation precisely because it would not work. Capital seldom views nationalisation with glee. But it has been known to accept it if there was an advantage to the private sector in doing so. Most of the state takeovers instituted by 1945–51 Labour government are good examples.

If capital believed that Holland's programme of national-isations would bring the benefits he claims, then it might regard the price as acceptable. But it fears that because the programme would not dynamise the private sector, it would lead to widespread demands for more nationalisation.

Nationalisation must form a part of any strategy for resolving the crisis in the interest of the working class. But its role should be to protect jobs in moves towards a fully, democratically planned socialist economy. Selective nationalisation will not restore competitiveness to an economy which remains pre-dominantly capitalist.

Public ownership of the financial institutions

The nationalisation of major banks and insurance companies is an important piece of unfinished business for the labour movement. The 1931 party conference unanimously passed a resolution calling for the nationalisation of banks and the direction of investment. Banking was the only major sector listed in Labour's 1945 nationalisation programme which stayed in private hands, when only the Bank of England was taken over. And the 1976 Labour Party conference overwhelmingly endorsed the policy.

The most important proposal in the 1976 statement calls for: 'A major publicly-owned stake in the financial system comprising the top seven insurance companies [sufficient to account for 30 per cent of premium income], a merchant bank and the four major private clearing banks [Barclays, Lloyds, Midland and National Westminster].'

The principal weakness of the statement is that it exaggerates what could be achieved *simply* by taking over the banks. It stresses the low rate of investment in British industry, and argues that the key to raising it 'lies in developing a publicly-owned stake in the very areas of the financial system where critical lending and invest-ment decisions are made: the banks and the insurance companies'.

But channelling more funds in capital's direction will not necessarily make it invest. The banks' evidence to the Wilson Committee in 1977 pointed out that manufacturing industry was borrowing less than half of what the banks had made available to them. The CBI commented that:

The clear conclusion of an overwhelming majority of our members is that it has not been a shortage of external finance [for example bank credit] that has restricted industrial investment but rather a lack of confidence that industry will be able to earn a sufficient return.

Nor would nationalising the banks and insurance companies be a way of gaining real control over industry. The insurance companies do have shareholdings in many major industrial firms. The Prudential, for example, holds more than 1 per cent of the shares of 35 of the largest 50 companies. But this is nowhere near control. The situation is quite different from that in Portugal, after April 1974, where bank nationalisations gave the government control over much of industry. In the UK banks lend to industry rather than owning it.

Democratic planning of the economy is inconceivable without government control of the financial system, so the demand for its nationalisation is a vital plank in any viable working-class programme. But it is no magic device for compelling capital to invest if it does not want to.

Planning agreements

A system of planning agreements would, so the plan goes, make companies invest when they would otherwise not do so. Companies would have to disclose a great deal more information than at present to the government and trade unions. Holland would want disclosed past levels and planned trends of turnover, investment and profits for each main product (information seldom available in published accounts), trade with subsidiaries abroad, extent of government assistance received, management salaries and fringe benefits (including private health arrangements, mortgage benefits, stock option schemes), wages by work category and plant, advertising expenditure and main suppliers and purchasers. This is the kind of information which has traditionally been associated with 'opening the books' to expose capitalist corruption and manipulation, to arm trade unionists for negotiation, to educate workers in the workings of the system and to expose capital's inability to develop production geared to social need.

But the idea is not simply to expose capital, but to brief

government which would then persuade companies to carry out policies – notably investment programmes – which they would otherwise reject as unprofitable. How?

Holland has four suggestions. One is to threaten that a nationalised company will take up the project if the private one does not. But why a company thus threatened should worry is unclear. If its investment analysts recommend against a venture, there are probably good reasons.

Holland also suggests that the government could publish details of its plan and of an unco-operative company's attitude. The victim might not welcome this, but could counter accusations of inadequate investment by pointing out that it did not regard the project as profitable, had a responsibility to its share-holders and so on. Bad publicity alone is highly unlikely to persuade firms to act unprofitably.

Another ploy would be to withhold government financial assistance, presumably including loans from the nationalised banking sector. Labour's 1976 programme suggests a similar use of price controls (probably the idea is to agree to price rises only if the company invests).

Finally, Holland argues that recalcitrant companies could be nationalised if all else failed. Labour's 1976 plan also mentions direct government control by issuing companies with directives and appointing official trustees to assume temporary control.

If capital meekly accepted these measures, particularly direct controls, the government would indeed be able to ensure a high level of investment. But Holland himself doubts whether capital would be so co-operative. 'A government bill requiring leading private companies to expand would be likely to result in at least widespread non-co-operation, if not a capital strike . . .' (Holland, p. 186).

And what would stop an investment strike? Holland has the only suggestion we know of – the use of nationalised firms. Although the argument is not spelled out, the idea is presumably that capital would fear that nationalised firms might gain markets at their expense, and would therefore not strike. But this view is naive in the extreme.

With the government issuing directives, appointing official trustees and nationalising firms which refused to fall into line, capital's priority would be to defend its control over production, leaving worries about market shares for another day. So it would try to disrupt the government's attempts to curtail its power. It would cease investment, cut back on production, refuse to release essential stocks, ship assets abroad and whatever else it deemed necessary. The result would be economic and social chaos. Capital will not give up control over economic activity without a fight.

Any government committed to maintaining a substantial capitalist sector would at this stage be forced to retreat. It would have no choice but to stop interfering in capital's affairs in exchange for continued production, which only capital could ensure as long as it owned and controlled the means of production.

Increased government regulation of private industry must feature in any economic strategy for the labour movement. It has an essential role in a transition from an anarchic, crisis-ridden capitalist market to a democratically planned socialist economy. But advocates of the planning-agreement system are badly mistaken in believing that capital would act against its own interests to fit in with a plan devised to protect those of workers.

The strategy's ideas for remedying problems in the production of surplus value are all inadequate. The strategy cannot defend workers' immediate interests and restore the conditions for sustained economic growth. The two objectives are incompatible so long as capital owns and controls the means of production.

Selective import controls

The proposal for selective import controls is a relatively recent addition to the AES. It emerged at about the time of the December 1976 IMF loan, but is now supported by all prominent strategy advocates.

Import controls are probably the most contentious component of the strategy within the left. Supporters claim they are essential to independence from such guardians of capitalist principles as the IMF and point out that direct control of foreign trade is practised by all countries which have broken from the capitalist bloc. Opponents argue they are a violation of class internationalism, because they seek to protect markets for UK capital and jobs for UK workers at the expense of jobs abroad.

It is in some ways unfortunate that argument about the AES within the labour movement has concentrated on import controls to such an extent. Their advocates do not claim that quotas for imports would in themselves solve any fundamental difficulties, but merely argue that controls would protect the strategy from severe balance of payments problems.

Substantial expansion of the economy would increase demand for imports, and reduce the incentive for firms to export. The resulting strain on the balance of payments would force the government to halt the expansion. Enter import controls. Their advantage over the more conventional response of devaluation is supposed to be that they would not automatically raise the price of imports, which would cause conditions for producing surplus value to deteriorate and set off a wage/price spiral.

There are three points against this claim. First, quotas would in fact lead to higher prices. Foreign capital would no longer have an incentive to undercut UK firms to expand market shares, and would raise prices. Workers would be compelled to switch from foreign goods to more expensive domestic substitutes. Finally, with foreign competition reduced, UK capital would raise prices. So controls would reduce real wages in a way similar to devaluation.

Secondly, controls on the scale required would almost certainly prompt retaliation. Countries whose exports to the UK were cut would place controls on imports from the UK. So UK exports would fall alongside imports and the balance of payments would not improve. The international crisis would be intensified by the contraction in world trade. Intense protectionism and a slump would be on the cards.

International reaction to the temporary import surcharge imposed by the 1964–70 Labour government showed clearly the danger of retaliation. Wilson has this to say of the situation one month after the surcharge was introduced:

On the night of Thursday, 1 November, I had an emergency, almost panic call from Patrick Gordon Walker in Geneva. He needed my clearance for a firm assurance that the 15 per cent import surcharge would be reduced in a matter of months. Otherwise the discussions would break down and country after country would be likely to retaliate against our trade. (Wilson, p. 35)

He was compelled to drop the surcharge within two years.

The surcharge was a feeble measure, calculated to have reduced imports by a mere £100m or so a year, imposed while the capitalist world was still enjoying an unprecedented boom. The AES calls for far tougher restrictions (*Tribune* talks of cutting imports by £3000m a year) to be imposed at a time of international crisis. Retaliation would be brutal.

Some Tribunites argue that foreign capital would not be any more bothered by import controls than by deflation, which would also cut imports.

But this is quite wrong. International capital expects deflation in response to crisis; it is the conventional way to restore adequate conditions for producing surplus value, at the expense of workers' jobs and living standards.

Import controls, on the other hand, would be viewed as avoiding the kind of attack on the working class needed to restore competitiveness. The UK would be seen as trying to solve its problems at the expense of foreign rivals, in a manner threatening international stability.

Even if import controls could work they would still not render the strategy as a whole viable. They would at best deal only with balance of payments problems, hardly the fundamental difficulty.

A wealth tax

Supporters of the strategy do not claim that a wealth tax would play any significant role in restoring conditions for sustained growth. Rather, it is intended to reduce the wealth of the capitalist class (and, some would say, 'pave the way' for socialism).

The 1974 Green Paper proposed a tax with rates beginning at 1 per cent on wealth in excess of £100,000 and rising to either $2\frac{1}{2}$ or 5 per cent on assets exceeding £5m. These rates are not high enough to reduce either luxury consumption or share holdings. But suppose the government introduced a tax which would substantially reduce share holdings, and hence the private ownership of industry. The ruling class would simply refuse to co-operate. Capital will not relinquish ownership and control of industry just because the government asked politely. Only sharp expropriation, backed by measures to ensure that production goes on, can succeed.

Industrial democracy

A further proposal to reduce the power of capital and inject an element of 'socialism' into economic organisation is for an extension of what has come to be known as 'industrial democracy'. Labour's *Programme for Britain 1976* proposed that companies employing over 2,000 workers establish a Main Policy Board, of which half the places 'would be available for workers' representatives, elected through the recognised trade union machinery'. It also pointed out that: 'If a company decides on a five-year plan which involves running down its British operations, the first workers know about the plan is usually when the redundancies are announced. All that can be done, through collective bargaining, is to salvage a compensation agreement.' The implication is that a board half of whose members were workers would be better able to reach compromises on closures.

The scheme favours class collaboration because of conviction that the free market, tamed by the National Enterprise Board and planning agreements, can guarantee capitalism organised in the interests of society rather than profits.

We believe a half-way house between free enterprise and central planning is impossible. The strategy cannot guarantee full employment and rising living standards. So putting workers on management boards would involve them in agreeing to attacks on their own jobs, pay and conditions in the interests of capitalist viability.

Real workers' control would involve the shop-floor electing representatives to supervise, and if necessary veto, management action. Such bodies will be essential to maintain production while capital stages non-co-operation and sabotage, inevitable if its control over economic activity is seriously challenged.

Concluding remarks

The strategy amounts to grafting weakened pieces of socialism on to sturdy, capitalist stock (see comparison below). It would not work – the system needs more thorough root and branch treatment.

'Alternative Strategy'	Socialist Plan
expand the economy/ maintain social programmes/ cut defence/35-hour week	production for need rather than profit
incomes policy/price controls	planned growth of incomes
nationalisation of banks	state monopoly of credit
import controls	state monopoly of foreign trade
selective nationalisation/ planning agreements	nationalisation of the monopolies/socialist plan of production
wealth tax	expropriation of the capitalists/ compensation according to need
industrial democracy	workers' control and management

The strategy is fatally flawed because it could surmount problems in the production of surplus value only by measures unacceptable to capital. Capitalists would resist immediately it started to bite, and could cause massive disruption because the bulk of production would remain under their control.

How do supporters of the strategy deal with this objection? The Communist Party's *British Road to Socialism* has the following to say:

> The fierce resistance to this policy which would come from the monopolists and bankers at home and abroad would have to be met by mobilising wide popular support for it on the basis of full

democratic discussion at every level in society . . . The right of the democratically elected government to carry out its programme would be firmly maintained. Concentrating the measures on nationalisation on the main monopoly groups would create possibilities for dividing the capitalist class and preventing united capitalist counteraction. (Communist Party, p. 40)

The idea that 'united capitalist counteraction' could be deflected by splitting the ruling class is absurdly optimistic. Capital stitched up in compulsory planning agreements and threatened by nationalisation would resist yielding autonomy and control just as aggressively as companies singled out for immediate state take-over. Not to do so would amount to class suicide.

What about mobilisation of 'wide popular support' and the 'right of the democratically elected government to carry out its programme'? Emphasising legal 'rights' to impose such policies might help win support from the wavering, but it would be catastrophic to rely on such rights. Capital would have no qualms about ditching democratic procedures if necessary, and its resistance could be countered only by workers acting together. Appeals to democracy or 'fairness' would not impress the opposition.

It is absolutely essential to mobilise a broad mass of workers. In fact, it is the only reliable safeguard against capitalist sabotage and reaction. But to be effective, such action must neutralise the opposition as quickly and completely as possible. To pass a law declaring that capital forfeits control of economic activity while leaving it to operate the real levers of economic power, control over means of production, is about as sensible as accepting the formal surrender of an army without confiscating its weaponry.

Many AES policies do have a place in a programme to build mass workers organisations. (Of those discussed above, the only ones to which we are opposed in the present context are import controls, incomes policies and worker participation.)

The demands for selective nationalisations and for planning agreements are sometimes denounced on the left as new ways of using state intervention to restructure British capitalism and improve its economic performance. Some strategy proponents do indeed support this project and suggest that the strategy would make capital act in both its own and workers' interests. But most supporters see the strategy as an attempt to control big business and force it to do whatever is necessary to provide jobs, social services and so forth, regardless of profitability. It is wrong to underestimate the political significance of support for such policies. Nevertheless, the strategy is misconceived because anti-capitalist policies do not stand a chance while the ruling class owns most of industry. To view its 'half-way house' arrangements as transitional to the type of programme required is a mistake too.

A transition to disaster, perhaps. Capitalist sabotage and disruption could discredit socialist ideas. The resulting economic chaos could pave the way for a reactionary takeover in which independent working-class organisations would be crushed. The 1973 coup in Chile, against an elected government pledged to a programme similar to the strategy, provides a bloody object lesson in this regard.

The economic possibilities of socialism

In this section we argue the economic case for a planned socialist economy. This is not to suggest that the only gains from socialism would be narrowly economic. Far from it. Nor are we seeking to provide a detailed blueprint for a socialist economy. Our case is that a planned socialist economy could, unlike the alternative strategy, protect workers' immediate interests and re-establish conditions for sustained economic growth.

The extent of nationalisation required

A planned economy would initially need only a relatively small number of companies nationalised. The largest 100 manufacturing companies account for nearly half of all manufacturing output and the largest 200 for about 60 per cent. Drawing the net rather wider to include commercial and property companies (see table 2, p. 165).

Further, the extent to which these giant companies exercise control is underestimated if one considers only their shares of output or assets. Many smaller firms function almost entirely as component suppliers or retailers for the giants. Thus the big car companies effectively determine the operations of smaller engineering companies, which supply components, and of car distributors. The giant chain stores exercise a similar control over numerous small consumer-good producers. Marks and Spencers, for example, has a reputation for exercising particularly tight control over many small textile companies.

There is a similar concentration in the financial sector. Twenty-five financial institutions (excluding insurance companies) control about 90 per cent of the assets of the largest 100. The 10 biggest insurance companies account for about two-thirds of the industry.

2: Assets of Top UK Companies in 1977

No. of companies	Proportion of total UK company assets %
20	21
50	33
100	44
250	59

Source: calculated from Trade and Industry,
17 November 1978.

All major sectors are dominated by this group of great corporations. The nationalisation of, say 200 industrial, commercial and financial giants would therefore be sufficient to ensure effective state control over economic activity.

There is nothing sacrosanct or magical about the figure 200 – 150 or 300 would achieve fundamentally the same effect: the state would control the major share of production. The takeover of 150 or more companies would deprive capital of the main levers of economic power. Meeting the AES target of 20–25 would not.

A socialist government would not automatically nationalise the *largest* 200 companies. Control of the London Brick Company, for example, narrowly outside the top 200, would be more useful in planning the economy than would Nestlés. There would have to be a judicious choice to provide the basis for effective planning.

Is planning practicable?

But how would such planning work? Is it practicable in a system as complex as the UK economy?

As Marx pointed out a hundred years ago, it is often the very people who extol the organisational excellence within capitalist enterprises, and nowadays recommend the excellence of corporate planning techniques, who most strenuously deny the possibility of applying the same techniques to co-ordinate production between enterprises. If General Motors can successfully plan its world-wide operations, why could not a workers' government use similar techniques to plan the UK economy?

General Motors sets production targets for its various models and then works out the implications, in terms of components production, employment and so on, for the detailed operation of its numerous plants. In broad terms, the same approach can be applied to planning the UK economy.

The starting point would be a conscious political decision about how much of production is to be made available for consumption and how much devoted to investment. The implications of the balance for individual sectors would then be worked out using input-output analysis (a device which shows the extent to which the output of one industry functions as inputs into another).

These calculations would yield production targets for the giant enterprises which dominate each sector, and these targets would in turn provide the basis for output levels for smaller component suppliers. The output targets would provide the data from which to calculate the labour and imported materials needed.

This account of the planning mechanism is obviously highly simplified. But it illustrates the basic point that no intractable technical problems are involved. The development in the last half century of techniques such as linear programming, a device for maximising chosen variables (such as output) subject to existing constraints (such as availability of labour and materials), and of equipment such as computers has rendered planning possible to a degree of sophistication our grandparents would have found almost inconceivable. Nor is it necessary to argue solely in terms of what could in principle be achieved. The experience of the USSR, in which production grew six and a half times between 1913 and 1965, and of capitalist economies in wartime has shown clearly the technical efficiency of planning.

Can planning be democratic?

Many people would concede the practical efficiency of planning but argue that it is inconsistent with democracy – attempts to establish planned socialist economies seem necessarily to degenerate into bureaucracy and repression. The Soviet Union is cited as evidence. It is true that the USSR has experienced such degeneration. But it is wrong to conclude on the basis of this, or a handful of other experiences, that democratic control of planning is impossible.

The details of democratic planning in the UK will necessarily be shaped by the form workers' institutions take in the fight to wrest control of the economy from capital. All we can offer here is a sketch to demonstrate that workers' democracy and planning are not inherently incompatible.

A socialist plan can be formulated democratically only by a workers' government – one composed of representatives elected and subject to recall by rank and file workers' bodies, and paid no more than those whom they represent.

The government would draw up national planning targets. Their details and implementation at industry level could be the responsibility of committees composed of workers in the industry concerned, workers in other sectors, as consumers of the products at home or work, and government representatives with the interest of the economy as a whole to protect. The plan could be supervised at plant level by workers' control over technical specialists and over issues such as hiring, firing and safety. The specific form of control would depend on the historical traditions of the workers' organisations in each industry and on the evolution of practices such as hiring and firing during the struggle to dislodge local representatives of capital.

Such a structure of planning and control is no more complex than many that already exist under capitalism. The principles of democratic control involved are ones which have a long history in the labour movement. The degree of rank and file involvement and vigilance essential to avoid degeneration has frequently been achieved during high points of working-class struggle. It is in any case inconceivable that the overthrow of capital would occur without massive involvement of workers.

What planning could achieve

Could a democratically controlled, planned socialist system in the UK restore the conditions for sustained growth while protecting workers' immediate economic interests? The present situation is characterised by a low rate of potential surplus value and profit. How could a socialist system which inherited these problems from capitalism avoid the same consequences?

To begin with, planning would allow a workers' government to avoid the difficulties giving rise to crisis. Once investment decisions were taken out of capital's hands, the fact that production yielded only a small surplus for accumulation would no longer lead to economic disruption. It would imply only that the potential rate of accumulation was severely constrained.

But the constraint would nevertheless present apparent difficulties for our claim that socialist planning could protect workers' interests and re-establish conditions for sustained growth. If accumulation and the rate at which output grew were sluggish, then the growth achieved would be relatively unimpressive and the scope for improving living standards initially severely limited. Given difficulties and disruption in seizing control of the economy and establishing planning, the claim seems too grand.

One way in which potential 'socialist stagnation' might be avoided is by diverting resources from uses which benefit neither workers' living standards nor accumulation. Luxury goods intended for capitalists would be a good place to start. One way in which a socialist programme would drastically reduce luxury consumption would be by paying no compensation to major shareholders, though safeguarding small savings invested in large companies mainly through pension funds and insurance companies.

It is notoriously difficult to calculate how much the rich spend on luxuries. The figures for their incomes do not tell the whole story, especially in respect of capital gains, the main route to wealth. Companies do not systematically publish details of fringe benefits, and we do not know how much individuals on high incomes save. A rough indirect estimate suggests that luxury consumption could account for up to 5 per cent of total production.

It seems likely that at least 5 per cent of resources would be required to eliminate pockets of poverty, so banning luxury consumption would hardly be enough to ensure that socialist planning could live up to our claims for it.

Other activities which absorb resources under capitalism but would be unnecessary under socialism could go as well. Some of the more obvious are:

- Costs of maintaining capitalist competition (duplication of product ranges).
- Costs of the capitalist financial system.
- Costs of maintaining work discipline (industrial relations departments) and costs of stifling the creative potential of the workforce. (Compare the workers' plan for Lucas Aerospace with the company's own ideas.)

It is not possible to estimate reliably the extent of the gains from eliminating waste. In the end they will be big, but it is important not to go overboard about the immediate benefits.

Consider the duplication of financial services. It would be foolish to implement widespread rationalisation of the banking system immediately after nationalising the major banks. This move would only mean large-scale unemployment among bank staff, hardly likely to strengthen their support for socialist transformation.

It would be necessary to provide in advance for alternative employment. An important aspect of the superiority of socialist planning is its ability to do this. But the process does take time.

The other side of the coin to the elimination of capitalist waste is the cost of democratic socialist planning. The planning machinery will absorb resources. For example, many ex-bank workers will be redeployed in local planning offices where their skill and training will be relevant. The operation of workers' control will also involve costs.

In the long run, there is little doubt that the resources

released by the elimination of capitalist waste will more than compensate for those absorbed into newly-created structures for planning and workers' control. But making resources available will take time, while the need for them will be high immediately – probably higher at first than later since there will inevitably be mistakes due to inexperience. In the short run, then, there probably will not be much in the way of resources released for accumulation or higher living standards.

So what would the advantage of democratic socialist planning be? Where would the planners find the resources to avoid 'socialist stagnation' at first? The answer lies in ending unemployment.

About one worker in 10 is currently without a job (see Chapter 4). But the loss of potential output is considerably more than 10 per cent because average labour productivity falls when unemployment sets in.

Many jobs are related only loosely to production levels. If markets fall by, say, 10 or 20 per cent, then many companies are unable to make any significant cuts in non-production workers, such as office and sales staff. The switchboard, for example, must be attended during office hours whether or not sales are flourishing. A growing number of direct production jobs are also relatively protected from fall-offs in sales. Many nineteenth century factories employed large numbers of workers in relatively few tasks. So it was fairly easy for capital to cut employment when sales fell. But much production today involves complex processes; each worker represents an essential cog in the machinery. Remove it and the entire mechanism stops.

Even if this is not the case, job losses are frequently prevented because workers object to them. UK capital has conspicuously failed to rationalise the use of existing plant as effectively as its international rivals in recent years (see Chapter 4). Resistance from the workforce is the most plausible explanation.

So higher employment would be accompanied by a rise in average labour productivity; output would go up by more than employment – past experience suggests by about twice as much. In other words, 10 per cent unemployment means a loss of production of about 20 per cent.

The results of a detailed survey for different industries

confirm how much more each could be producing (Table 3). Though the figures were compiled in 1977, the basic picture has not changed.

3: Potential Increases in Output

	With present hours %	With additional overtime %	With additional labour %
Food, drink and tobacco	6.3	11.0	15.5
Chemicals	16.9	18.2	19.5
Mechanical engineering	13.6	21.5	35.0
Motors	1.4	6.7	33.6
Metals	6.0	10.6	11.5
Textiles	7.4	13.0	18.8
Clothing and footwear	15.0	20.8	24.5
Paper and printing	13.4	22.4	28.3
Construction	14.9	22.2	36.0
Total	7.6	12.4	21.5

Source: National Institute Economic Review, *February 1977.*

It may be worth spelling out just what a 20 per cent loss of production means, in more down to earth terms. Full employment would permit the production of about £43.5bn extra goods and services per year (at 1980 prices). This production could provide the following improvements:

	1980 prices £ billion
Consumption by those currently out of work, who would then be employed	8.9

50 per cent increase in pensions and other social security benefits (less saving of unemployment benefit, and half supplementary benefit)	6.7
Minimum full-time earnings of £105 per week (men and women)	12.8
75 per cent increase of house-building	5.2
Increase of 25 per cent in expenditure on health and education	5.3
50 per cent increase in manufacturing and construction investment	4.5
Total	43.4

Source: National Income and Expenditure *1979 edition and* Department of Employment Gazette, *October 1978, p. 1160. Figures at 1978 prices have been increased by 33 per cent to allow for estimated inflation between 1978 and 1980. The cost of £105 minimum earnings was based on April 1978 earnings figures, and an £80 minimum earnings target which was then increased to allow for 33 per cent inflation.*

These items are not alternatives. They could all be achieved simultaneously.

Those who doubt the technical possibility of obtaining this additional output usually suggest one of two supposed economic difficulties. The first concerns financing. Where would the money come from? 'Could the country afford it?'

Yes – the state could simply print the money required to circulate the extra output. This would not be inflationary, because increased spending would be balanced by more goods and services available. So the government would print money to pay the wages of those previously unemployed, who would spend it on some of the extra goods then available in the shops. The money would return to the government. That part of additional output would go to the people who produced it – the workers. Some of it would also go to pensioners as the government put up pensions. Again, the extra cash would return to the government. As long as additional purchasing power is kept in line with extra production, there will not be inflation.

The second doubt concerns the balance of payments. Would it be possible to sell sufficient exports to pay for necessary imports? Under capitalism, after all, an increase in domestic incomes usually means a rise in imports without a corresponding one in exports. Because most decisions about buying and selling abroad are made privately, there is no reason why they should balance out.

But under a socialist plan, control of giant companies and the banking sector would give the government almost total control of foreign trade. Goods could be directed into exports and unnecessary imports prevented to ensure a workable balance. Both objections are therefore unfounded.

Our list of what a planned economy could produce is one way of expressing the costs of unemployment. It is a narrowly economic, minimum estimate of the price the working class is currently paying to keep an outmoded system. As such, it provides an excellent argument for socialism.

It would of course be difficult to implement a socialist plan. There would inevitably be mistakes in democratic planning at first; and companies not immediately nationalised would be in a position to cause considerable difficulties unless rigorously controlled by their employees.

Nor would difficulties be restricted to internal developments. The technical issue of balancing foreign trade would present no great problems. But external relations generally would almost certainly involve trade boycotts, and indeed sabotage, from foreign capital.

But mistakes and sabotage are unlikely to lead to a shortfall in output to match the current 20 per cent, let alone the proportions that could be reached under Thatcher. The UK's integration into the world-capitalist market has after all, already brought the country to the verge of being incapable of maintaining a significant manufacturing sector.

The Alternative Economic Strategy promises improvements,

while not disrupting present economic arrangements as thoroughly as a genuine socialist plan would. But it has a fatal flaw. It fails to acknowledge the political need to launch a decisive attack on the power of capital if investment and production are to be planned in the interests of workers. This could have potentially disastrous consequences for the working class. If the left tried an AES-type programme and lost, the capitalist class would not hesitate to consolidate its victory. A defeat would leave the labour movement vulnerable to vicious economic and political attacks.

The broadest possible mobilisation of workers, both at home and abroad, would be needed to launch a successful socialist programme and to nurse it through initial difficulties. There is not widespread support for such an approach at present. But Alternative Economic Strategy supporters who oppose putting forward an extensive nationalisation programme on the grounds that it sounds too much like socialism display only contempt for the labour movement.

Nationalisation must be presented in the context of a coherent socialist programme. Widespread support for it would have to be sought persistently and persuasively. The labour movement could launch the necessary campaign. And it *is* necessary; the programme is the only one which could protect workers' immediate and long-term interests. To shirk the challenge because the approach sounds too radical is the worst kind of political defeatism.

Appendix: The Profits Squeeze

This appendix examines further the facts of the decline in profitability that occurred in the advanced capitalist world from the late 1960s onwards and the forces responsible for it. It begins with a brief outline of what is probably the orthodox marxist explanation for it then discusses our own interpretation, that of over-accumulation in relation to the supply of labour, in more detail, with reference to points emphasised by other writers.

The law of the tendency of the rate of profit to fall

Marxists usually explain declining profitability in general as being due to the operation of what Marx called 'the law of the tendency of the rate of profit to fall' (LTRPF). The theory is complex, and subject to differing interpretations. But the essential idea is as follows.

On the one hand, the development of capitalist production involves systematic increases in the quantity of means of production (machinery etc.) used by each worker. On the other hand, only labour produces surplus value, which is the source of profit. So, even if the amount of surplus value produced by each worker tends to rise somewhat with increased labour productivity, it nevertheless falls in proportion to the increasing value laid out by capitalists on new means of production. Since the rate of profit is surplus value divided by the value of means of production, the rate of profit must therefore fall.

Advocates of the LTRPF mistakenly assume that an increase in the physical mass of capital operated by each worker (the technical composition of capital) necessarily implies a rise in its *value* relative to the value of either output or surplus. Marx himself was well aware that increasing productivity would cheapen machinery and raw materials. But he regarded this cheapening as quantitatively less important than the build-up of the mass of means of production, and hence concluded that the value of fixed capital would rise over time. In fact these two tendencies, increasing mass of means of production and declining value of each item, have tended roughly to cancel each other out.

The following figures demonstrate that the mass of capital operated by each worker has not systematically grown faster than the productivity of labour in the post-war period. Thus the cost of means of production in terms of the labour time required to produce them (or to put it another way, the value of capital operated by each worker) has not generally increased. There has been a perceptible upward trend in the UK and W. Germany, but a downward one in Japan and Italy.

1: Rate of Accumulation and Devaluation of Capital: Industry, 1953–72

	Rates of growth				
	(1) capital stock	(2) employ- ment	(3) capital per worker (1)–(2)	(4) productivity (devaluation of capital)	(5) value of capital per worker (3)–(4)
	Average annual percentages				
France	5.8	1.0	4.8	5.4	—0.6
Germany	7.0	1.0	6.0	5.0	1.0
Italy	6.6	1.8	4.8	5.0	—0.2
Japan	12.5	3.7	8.8	8.9	—0.1
UK	4.2	0	4.2	3.0	1.2
USA	3.3	0.9	2.2	2.7	—0.5

Source: See Table 3 of Chapter 2.

The explanation for the general fall in the rate of profit from the mid-sixties cannot therefore be the operation of the LTRPF.

Profit rates and profit shares

The key to understanding the decline in the rate of profit over the last 10–15 years lies in recognising that capitalists have been receiving a declining *margin* of profit on sales; that is, the *share* of profits in the value of output has fallen. This phenomenon has become known as the 'profits squeeze'. This development is illustrated in a particularly sharp way by the following figures for the profit margin in manufacturing industry: the percentage of profit in each pound (or dollar, etc.) of sales.

2: Manufacturing Profit, 1951–77

	Percentage of value of output					
	1951	1960	1970	1973	1975	1977
Italy	25.2	16.5	19.6	3.6	−3.3	0
Germany	34.4	29.3	20.6	13.6	11.0	11.8
Japan	36.3*	43.7	39.3	29.2	15.5	16.6
USA	25.9	19.6	16.2	17.7	17.5	18.6
UK	30.8	27.4	16.1	17.7	4.7	9.6

Source: National income statistics for individual countries

*1954 figure

The decline in profit margins means, as a matter of arithmetic, that the cost of employing labour has risen, in real terms, more than the productivity of labour has. In turn, the decline in margins has reduced the profit rate.

The explanation based on the LTRPF is in our view wrong. But is nevertheless based on an important and correct notion at the centre of Marx's thought, and absent from some accounts of the profits squeeze: the idea that the root of the problem is too much accumulation.

Over-accumulation in relation to the labour supply

The basic account of over-accumulation given in Chapter 1 – excess demand for labour generating a rapid rise in real wages as capitalists bid against each other to obtain labour to operate newly-installed machinery – implicitly assumed a constant price level (or one determined exclusively by monetary conditions and unaffected by labour-market developments). The significance of this assumption is that it implies that a faster increase in *money* wages is also a faster increase in *real* wages. It is, of course, higher real wages which provoke additional scrapping and ensure the transfer of sufficient labour to operate all new equipment.

But suppose the government responds to the rise in wages which accompanies the onset of over-accumulation by expanding the money supply rapidly. Easy credit could encourage capitalists to maintain the rate of accumulation, despite increased wage costs. Workers paid more spend more, increasing total demand for commodities. If all productive capital is in use, so that output cannot be raised, increased demand will put up prices. Bigger money wages are offset by higher prices, so real wages stay where they were.

If real wages do not rise, scrapping is slow and capitalists continue to have difficulty finding enough workers to operate all newly-installed machinery. Demand for labour becomes more intense. Wage increases tend to swell, because workers and capitalists anticipate further price rises. If money wages are to grow faster without giving workers real wage rises, then credit and prices must grow even faster as well. Thus, if as a result of capitalists' accumulation decisions and government credit policy, over-accumulation fails to generate the 'necessary' increase in real wages, the result is rising inflation.

When this process begins to get out of hand, and governments fear the social and political effects of accelerating price rises, credit policy may be sharply reversed. This may well precipitate a collapse of investment, made more likely by real wages failing to rise so that there is potentially profitable capacity around which capitalists have been unable to find labour to operate. If prices cannot be brought down, then the collapse in investment may well reduce total demand below the level required to maintain full employment.

The fall in demand and reduction in the rate of inflation will permit a real wage increase, made 'necessary' by the onset of over-accumulation, to occur, and hence profits will fall. Profits will also fall further if a recession develops, idle capacity grows and prices are cut as the struggle for markets intensifies. This fall in profits as a result of the reversal of earlier expansionary policies is emphasised by Rowthorn. In this situation the fall in profits appears to be caused by the tightening of credit and onset of recession. In reality, though, this just makes worse what is fundamentally caused by the prior over-accumulation. In our view events in the late sixties and the early seventies corresponded to such a pattern.

Thus far in the Appendix trade unions have implicitly been treated simply as channels through which the money wage increases 'required' by the demand and supply situation in the labour market are transmitted. But it is perfectly possible that the strength and militancy of the labour movement is such that the money wage increases won in a situation of over-accumulation exceed those 'required'. Such wage explosions can boost inflation as governments expand credit to allow prices to catch up with wages.

Further, wage explosions – or a more gradual acceleration of money-wage settlements – may occur before a labour shortage bites. A reduction in unemployment and general tightening of labour markets may give trade unions the confidence and strength to win larger money wage increases before such increases are 'required'. This can be considered either as 'anticipation' of over-accumulation or as 'social and institutional' over-accumulation – in excess of that which the system can sustain without either falling profits or inflation, given the strength of the labour movement. The money wage increases could be absorbed through inflationary state policies, but the alarm and uncertainty created by wage explosions and accelerating inflation may tend to a rapid move to deflationary policies and thus to squeezed profits.

This is to some extent what happened in the post-war period. Italy in the early sixties and again in the late sixties is perhaps the best example. It is this aspect of the overall process which was emphasised by Glyn and Sutcliffe. We would stress the underlying and central role of accumulation and the sense in which such developments can be understood as a social and institutional anticipation of over-accumulation.

'Premature' gross wage increases of this type may be sparked off by a widening gap between pre- and post-tax wages as the rise in state spending requires a higher and higher proportion of workers' incomes to be taken in taxation. This factor may well have an important influence on wage demands in a number of countries. But note that it can only contribute to an explanation of the profit squeeze to the extent that the latter reflects the influence of deflationary state policies taken to damp down wage increases; otherwise there is no mechanism whereby bigger increases in gross *money* wages are translated into higher gross *real* wages.

Finally, the analysis so far has implicitly assumed fairly competitive product markets. In reality, of course, many large companies possess considerable market power. One important implication of this is that there may be machines which could be operated profitably at current wage and price levels but are left idle because the firm believes the extra output could not be sold without reducing prices and profits.

The average extent of such market power varies over time. Concentration within national economies, a process which tends to increase the extent of market power, has proceeded rapidly in the post-war period. But its effects have been more than offset by the rapid growth in international trade and investment. This tendency to increase international competition reduces the extent of market power and can erode profits independently of the scrapping mechanism and the demand for labour.

Undoubtedly this factor has been important for the weakest competitors, such as Britain, as we emphasised in Chapter 2. Even the stronger countries have not been immune, with the reduction of trade barriers, and especially when, as in recent years for W. Germany and Japan in particular, their exchange rates have moved sharply upwards. In most cases, however, in contrast to Glyn and Sutcliffe we feel that this aspect of the uneven development of the different capitalist countries has probably been secondary in importance to over-accumulation and shrinkage of the reserve army of labour.

References and Guide to Further Reading

Entries marked* bear most directly on the arguments in the text.

Armstrong, P. J., Glyn, A. J., Harrison, J. M. and Sutcliffe, R. B. 'Reconstruction – Metropolitan Capitalism from World War II to Korea', mimeo, Oxford 1976.

*Bacon, R. and Eltis, W. *Britain's Economic Problem: Too Few Producers*, London 1976.

Barratt-Brown, M. *From Labourism to Socialism*, London 1972.

*Beckerman, W. (ed.) *Slow Growth in Britain*, Oxford 1979.

*Blackaby, F. (ed.) 1978a, *De-Industrialisation*, London 1978.

*Blackaby, F. (ed.) 1978b, *British Economic Policy 1960–74*, Cambridge 1978.

Blackaby, F. 'Narrative 1960–74' and 'Incomes Policy' in Blackaby (ed.) 1978b, *op. cit.*

Boltho, A. *Japan: An Economic Survey*, Oxford 1975.

*Bosanquet, N. and Townshend, P. *Labour and Equality*, London 1980

*Boston Consulting Group, *Strategy Alternatives for the British Motorcycle Industry*, London 1975.

Buchan, A. *The Right to Work*, London 1972.

*Central Policy Review Staff, *The Future of the British Car Industry*, London 1975.

Confederation of British Industry, *The Road to Recovery*, London 1976.

Confederation of British Industry, *Economic Policy and Budget Representations to the Incoming Government*, London 1979.

Clark, T. A. and Williams, N. P. 'Measures of Real Profitability', *Bank of England Quarterly Bulletin*, December 1978.

*Coates, K. (ed.) *What Went Wrong?*, Nottingham 1979.

Communist Party, *British Road to Socialism*, London 1978.

Delestré, H. and Mairesse, H. *La Rentabilité des Sociétés Privées en France 1956–75*. INSEE, Paris 1977.

Department of Industry, *The Regeneration of British Industry*, Cmnd. 5710, London 1974.

Elliot, R. 'Industrial Relations and Manpower Policy' in Blackaby (ed.) 1978b, *op. cit.*

*Ellman, M. *Socialist Planning*, Cambridge 1979.

Evans, D. *While Britain Slept*, London 1975.

Fay, F. and Young, H. 'The Day the Pound Nearly Died', *Sunday Times*, 14, 21 and 28 May 1978.

Fay, F. and Young, H. 'The Fall of Heath', *Sunday Times*, 22 February, 29 February and 7 March 1976.

Feldstein, M. and Summers, L. 'Is the Rate of Profit Falling?', *Brookings Papers on Economic Activity*, 1977.

Freeman, C. 'Technical Innovation and British Trade Performance', in Blackaby (ed.) 1978a, *op. cit.*

Fua, G. *Formazione distribuzione e impiego del reddito del 1861: Sintesi Statistica*, Rome 1972.

*Glyn, A. J. and Sutcliffe, R. B. *British Capitalism Workers and the Profit Squeeze*, London 1972.

Gowland, D., *Monetary Policy and Credit Control*, London 1978.

*Hill, T. P. *Profits and Rates of Return*, OECD, Paris 1979.

*Holland, S. *The Socialist Challenge*, London 1975.

Holland, S., (ed.) *Beyond Capitalist Planning*, London 1979.

Hughes, J. 'The 35-hour Week' in Barratt Brown et al. (eds.) *Full Employment*, Nottingham 1978.

Hurd, D. *An End to Promises*, London 1979.

*Itoh, M. 'The Inflational Crisis of World Capitalism', in *Value and Crisis*, London 1980.

Joseph, K. *Conditions for Fuller Employment*, London 1978.

*Kawakami, T. 'The Crisis of the Capitalist World', *Cambridge Journal of Economics*, June 1979.

Labour Party, *Programme for Britain 1973*, London 1973.

Labour Party, *Programme for Britain 1976*, London 1976.

Maddison, A. 'Phases of Capitalist Development', *Banca Nazionale del Lavoro Review*, June 1977.

Maddison, A. 'The Long-run Dynamics of Productivity Growth', *Banca Nazionale del Lavoro Review*, March 1979.

*Mandel, E. *Late Capitalism*, London 1975.

*Mandel, E. *The Second Slump*, London 1978.

Milligan, A. *The New Barons*, London 1976.

Nordhaus, W. 'The Falling Share of Profits', *Brookings Papers on Economic Activity*, 1974.

*OECD, (1977), *Towards Full Employment and Price Stability*, Paris 1977.

Ohkawa, K. and Rosovsky, H. *Japanese Economic Growth*, Stanford 1973.

Phelps-Brown, E. H. 'Industrial Productivity and Real Wages', *Economic Journal*, March 1973.

*Phelps-Brown, E. H. 'What is the British Predicament?' *Three Banks Review*, December 1977.

Ramelson, R. *Bury the Social Contract*, London 1976.

*Robinson, H. L. 'The Downfall of the Dollar', *Socialist Register, 1973*, London 1974.

*Rowthorn, R. 'Mandel's Late Capitalism', *New Left Review*, No. 98, 1976.

Sedgemore, B. *The How and Why of Socialism*, Nottingham 1978.

Sewill, B. 'In Place of Strikes', in *British Economic Policy 1970–74 – Two Views*, London 1975.

Stout, D. K. 'De-Industrialisation and Industrial Policy', in Blackaby (ed.) 1978a, *op. cit.*

Stewart, M. *The Jekyll and Hyde Years*, London 1977.

Taylor, A. and Threadgold, M., *'Real' National Saving and its Sectoral Composition*, Bank of England Discussion Paper No. 6, London 1979.

H. M. Treasury, *Public Expenditure to 1978–9*, London 1975.

H. M. Treasury, *The Government's Expenditure Plans 1979–80 to 1982–83*, London 1979.

Weekes, R., et al. *Industrial Relations and the Law*, London 1975.

Wigham, E. *Strikes and the Government 1893–1974*, London 1976.

Wilson, H. *Labour Government 1964–70: A Personal Record*, London 1971.

Sources of Statistics

Many statistics used in the text are not specifically referenced.

These are the major sources:

Bank of England Quarterly Bulletin, London.
Bank for International Settlements Annual Report, Basle.
Cambridge Economic Policy Review, Cambridge, annually.
Economic Outlook, Paris O.E.C.D., twice yearly.
Economic Trends, London, monthly.
Department of Employment Gazette, London, monthly.
Monthly Digest of Statistics, London, monthly.
National Income and Expenditure, London, annually.
National Institute Economic Review, London, quarterly.
Trade and Industry, London, weekly.